Juan M. Alvarez

FENG SHUI:
THE HARMONY OF LIFE

Translation: Maggie Leyes

FAIRY'S RING
Miami, Florida

Feng Shui, The Harmony of Life
First Edition, June 1998
Published by Fairy's Ring, Inc.
Copyright by Juan M. Alvarez

Translation: Maggie Leyes

ISBN: 1-892231-01-8

Graphics design: Cover: Jorge M. Alvarez
               Illustrations: Juan M. Alvarez

Printed by
Trade Litho, Inc.
Miami, Florida

Professor **Thomas Lin Yun,** Grand Master of the Black Sect Tantric Buddhism, in its Fourth Level, dedicate his thoughts to all the readers. This blessing was written in Chinese calligraphy and cinnabar and blessed with a sacred mudra.

"On the lunar day, September 9, 1997, I dedicate with an infinite sutra, my friend's great book, Feng Shui, The Harmony of Life, blessing all the readers with prosperity, health and protection."

The Lin Yun Temple
2959 Russell Street, Berkely, CA 94705
510-841-2347 510-548-2621fax Website: www.yunlintemple.org

September 1996
The Author with Master Lin Yun in Tibet.

Dedication

This book is dedicated to my beloved wife, Carmen, whose help, support and devotion have been my constant inspiration.

I would also like to thank Katherine Metz and Melanie Lewandowski, advance students of Master Thomas Lin Yun, for sharing their knowledge of the legendary Chinese art of Feng Shui with me, and for their ongoing motivation and example.

This work is due to the spiritual guidance of Master Thomas Lin Yun, whose teachings have allowed me to draw closer to the divine light, the Spark of life, the universal creative force, Chi.

This book is also dedicated to all those men and women in this age of transformation, especially those readers I am sharing this ancestral knowledge with. Those who understand and use these traditional methods and techniques will pull back, if ever so slightly, the veil of illusion to bring light to the shadows of life and to improve their relationships, prosperity and health.

The practice of Feng Shui will enrich your lives, helping you merge with the energy that is the essence and the spirit of nature, through the universal principles of harmony and the sublime spiritual experiences you will undergo.

Om Ma Ni Pad Me Hum

PREFACE

The Harmony of Living

Many of my good friends and disciples, who have been studying Feng Shui and are Feng Shui experts, have often told me that if they ever publish a book they would want me to write a preface and do Chinese calligraphy as part of the illustrations. Of course, their request is out of friendship and respect for me as their teacher. Therefore, I am always delighted and touched when someone asks me to write a preface. Some, however, believe that a Feng Shui book with my preface, epilogue or Chinese calligraphy could further help them promote and sell their books.

Today, as I write this preface for Juan M. Alvarez for this Feng Shui book, "The Harmony of Life," I am deeply touched that this book is, in fact, in its 5th edition in less than one year of publishing. The success of this book has proven that a well-written book needs not rely on my preface for it to sell. I had promised Juan that I would write the preface for the book before the publication of its 1st edition. I did in fact start writing the preface for him, but I wanted to finish reading the book first. Since Juan's book is written in Spanish, I had to ask a friend to translate it for me. At the time I was involved in traveling around the world conducting speeches, lectures and workshops throughout Europe, Asia, America and Australia. As a result, I could not finish the preface on time for the publication of his 1st edition in April, 1997. For his 2nd edition, my amiable and honorable friend, Juan, again asked me sincerely and respectfully to write the preface for his book. I agreed to finish the preface on time. Now, Juan is ready to publish the 5th edition, and once again, he asked me to write the preface. This time, I was determined to finish the preface after returning to my Long Island Temple, from a

風水沿革

寺禪林豐敦題

The background and development of Feng Shui

long trip to Germany, France, Switzerland, and England. The whole story demonstrates Juan's loving heart, sincerity and respect for me as well as his persistent and patient spirit.

Juan's book is as well-written and perfect as it is; and such excellent book with truthful content need not rely on my preface and calligraphy to improve its sales and promotion. The publications of the 1st, 2nd, 3rd and 4th editions have already proven that his book is both accurate and substantial as well as easily understood and shall continue with 6th, 7th, etc. editions. The very reason why I insisted on finishing this preface is because I understand that Juan wants me to write this preface because of his sincerity and respect for me as well as our friendship and his genuine acknowledgement of the original source of knowledge.

The author, Mr. Alvarez, has indeed attended my workshops, lectures and speeches, furthermore, he has also studied the three classical books on Feng Shui written by Sarah Rossbach. He has physically participated in a grand Feng Shui observation and analysis as well as incense offering trip to China led by our very respectful Professor, Leo Chen. During this Feng Shui trip, we visited various famous mountains, temples, cities, and holy places. Thus, Juan not only has theoretical background, but also true life Feng Shui analysis experience from the China trip.

The book begins with the history of Feng Shui and discusses many practical applications on how to use Feng Shui for decoration. It clearly presents the Chinese philosophy on the I-Ching's eight trigrams and how it carries out the rationale of harmony between mankind and the universe.

This book also describes, by using the principles of Feng Shui and both mundane and transcendental cures, the Black Sect Tantric Buddhism's Feng Shui philosophy. In the last chapters of the book, the author clearly and accurately

住家的傳統風水解法

雲石居士林石敬題

introduces his readers the types of Chi in humans, the differentiation of the 5 elements of Chi and simple Chinese astrology. Even more admirable is that he has written a summary of key points and given a list of valuable references for different schools of Feng Shui.

If you pay special attention while reading this book, you will understand there are many different schools of Feng Shui, and that the school I have established, the Black Sect Tantric Buddhist Feng Shui School, has various methods of Feng Shui adjustment, including both exoteric and esoteric, for residential and commercial buildings, factories, airports, harbors, businesses, hospitals, companies, and urban planning. This book is especially honorable as the author not only clearly describes the ancient Chinese philosophy, i.e. the harmonious spirit of Yang within Yin and Yin within Yang presented in the I-Ching eight trigram. He also carefully analyzed the colors as well the relationship between interior and exterior aspects of eight trigrams.

This book has included very profound information. As for the practical aspects of Feng Shui, Juan gives concrete classifications on how to select lot, observe the shape of the lot and its surroundings, observe the Feng Shui in the neighborhood and influences from the community's environment, and how to recognize other details such as road and street, front door, master bedroom, kitchen stoves, beams, walls, staircases, and columns. In addition, he also discusses how to arrange furniture. He carefully explains the Black Sect Tantric Buddhist's minor adjustment methods for buildings that require transcendental Feng Shui cures. These minor adjustments including the use of mirrors, windchimes, flutes, crystal balls; etc. It also encompasses the research on the vitality of plants.

In addition, this book includes the most secretive parts of Feng Shui; that is, the transcendental cures, the so called

Dharma. These transcendental cures include the Three Secrets reinforcement, Tracing the Nine Star Path, Eight Door arrangement, how to conceive a child, interior/exterior Chi adjustment, how to clarify one's mind and heart, and methods on how to reach self-realization which include heart sutra meditation, the Sunshine Buddha meditation, prosperity exercise prosperity, the eight trigrams meditation, how to adjust one's luck, health, and mental and physical balance, and secret holistic healing that can enhance one's wisdom. From the power that created the universe, he brings the philosophy of eight trigrams, Taoism, Chi, Yin Yang, and five elements, and even includes the principles of "substance is void and void is substance," the three-color systems which include the colors of the five elements, the six-syllable mantra and the seven colors of the rainbow.

He also describes the five elements versus their corresponding personality. Though this book is on Feng Shui from the perspective of folkloric studies, it encompasses many different philosophical points of view of Black Sect Tantric Buddhism (BSTB). Juan's words at the end of this book are especially touching. I highly recommend this book to architects, doctors, teachers, psychologists, urban planners, landscapers, interior designers and all people who have or have not studied Feng Shui. I believe that everyone, regardless of their field shall benefit greatly from this book.

Prof. Thomas Lin Yun
Berkely, California.
March 2, 1998

An Urgent Case

It was 6 p.m. and I was finishing a Feng Shui seminar. I had to leave shortly for the Miami airport to pick up my son who was due in from New York at 9 p.m. While answering various questions, two students, Luis and Isabel approached me. They asked for my immediate help. They needed a Feng Shui consultation done on their business. I tried to arrange a visit for the next day, but they told me that tomorrow might be too late. They had just received an eviction notice for being behind in their rent, and with the financial straits they were in, they didn't feel they could stay open even two or three more days. They added that their sales were practically nil. As their case was so urgent, I agreed to go with them.

When we arrived, I found serious problems including how the furnishings were arranged, that the bathroom was located in the area of finances and that the front door was blocked by aggressive furnishings with sharp corners.

I rolled up my sleeves and with my friends' help, we began changing the furnishings around. We placed some floral arrangements and arranged the product displays artistically. We sealed the bathroom door with a transcendental solution, as there wasn't time to hang a mirror on the outside of the door. We balanced the colors. And we rearranged objects and rehung pictures, putting them in their corresponding areas. We placed purple in the finances area, red in the fame area and pink in the relationship area. We worked hard and before 9 p.m., we had made some real changes. We finished just in time for me to pick up my son.

At noon the next day, Isabel phoned us and was very pleased. On the way home the night before, they had stopped to buy a lottery ticket. That morning they found that theirs were among the winning numbers. It wasn't much money, but it was enough to pay the rent on their business. It was the first time in their lives they had won the lottery. And not only that, that same morning they had also signed two important contracts that would provide enough long term income that they could keep their business open.

Was it possible that energy, now flowing unimpeded through their business, had something to do with the sudden luck of the owners and the clients' behavior? Could the changes that we did the night before, following simple rules of Feng Shui, have had such remarkable results?

I

THE HISTORY OF FENG SHUI

The Transmission of the Legendary
Art of Feng Shui in the West

One of the first books on Feng Shui in the West was *The Science of the Sacred Landscape* written by the missionary, Ernest Eitel, and published in 1873. It aroused a certain curiosity in Europe, but not enough to popularize the art. A hundred years had to pass until this topic would again reach the attention of the western world. Sarah Rossbach, one of Master Thomas Lin Yun's students, wrote the book, *Feng Shui: The Chinese Art of Placement* in 1983. Written with wonderful simplicity, this work generated a lot of interest with the American public. Later, Sarah published two more books: *Interior Design with Feng Shui*, and *Living Color*, both under the guidance of Master Lin Yun. Of all the schools of Buddhism, the smallest and oldest is the Black Sect of Tantric Buddhism which has become the channel for transmitting the principles and methods of this millennia-old tradition to the modern world.

As I mentioned in the introduction, all the information about the traditional and transcendental methods of the legendary environmental art of Feng Shui in this book comes directly from the teachings of Master Thomas Lin Yun, the spiritual leader of the Black Sect of Tibetan Tantric Buddhism in its Fourth Level.

Master Thomas Lin Yun

In 1972, a Buddhist priest began visiting the United States teaching the environmental art of Feng Shui. Master Lin Yun began his studies in Tibetan Tantric Buddhism at the age of six. Born in China, he has spent his entire life studying Buddhism and the mystical art of Feng Shui. He is a simple man of few words whose look reflects the depth of his awareness, and whose life is a living example of dedication to spiritual work.

Master Lin Yun encourages his students to disseminate and share the knowledge and philosophy of Feng Shui - that he brought to the United States - with all those who are looking for greater peace and harmony in their lives.

Feng Shui

Modern technology and overpopulation have created large scale pollution problems that affect the natural vital cycles of the planet. These same problems are becoming increasingly more acute, creating serious environmental changes that are affecting our emotions, health, harmony and even life itself.

Feng Shui comes to us from a remote past as a tool we can use to bless, protect and harmonize the vital energy that flows through our being and is projected into our immediate surroundings, our homes and our work place. The environmental art of Feng Shui creates harmony in the buildings we have created and in the people who inhabit them.

The first steps of Feng Shui will bring us -through the depths of our own minds, ideas, beliefs and present reality- toward an understanding of a philosophy based on the universal principles of duality, the theory of Yin and Yang. We will begin walking the path of millennia-old understanding. We will learn to grasp certain principles manifested in nature: The Five Chinese Elements, The Constructive and Destructive Cycles of the Five Elements, The Three Schools of Colors, The Lines of Harmony (Ba-Gua) and the Projection and Movement of the Lines of Harmony. True understanding of these theories will awaken thoughts that have laid dormant since time immemorial. And through Feng Shui, we will develop a certain sensitivity to the energies that are present in our surroundings.

The Sect of Tantric Buddhism, in its Fourth Level, teaches us how to change our homes and our work places into a reflection of our lives and our hopes, and gives us the information we need to reinforce those areas of our lives that need adjustment. Feng Shui adjustments and arrangements are made using the Nine Minor Additions of the Tradition.

The mystical side of Feng Shui, known as the Transcendental Method, is the most important aspect of this system. Using this method produces results of 120%.

14

Feng Shui allows negative energy that affects our health, the economy and our personal relationships to be transformed into positive energy that creates prosperity, health and abundance both on the physical and spiritual levels.

The Meaning of Feng Shui

Literally the word Feng Shui means Air-Water. A synonym for Feng Shui is "Geomancy," although this term is more often associated with certain Arabic divinatory practices that spread throughout Europe during the Middle Ages. However, the word Geomancy was used by certain writers in the 18th century to refer to the art of Feng Shui.

Another name given to Feng Shui, that comes from ages past, is "Kan-Yu" which means "Embracing and Supporting" symbolizing Heaven (Embracing) and Earth (Supporting). This term comes from Taoist philosophy which relates the events of Earth with those of the Universe and what occurs in the Universe, with what is happening on Earth.

China is a predominantly agriculturally-based country. Through the centuries, Chinese agriculture has been able to preserve the fertility of its land and feed the largest population on Earth. They have succeeded by understanding and following the natural rhythms and elements of nature.

Many search for Shan-gri-la, others for a bit of heaven or a place of glory. The Chinese Feng Shui Masters, on the other hand, look for how to place objects, combine colors and their shapes to create harmonious surroundings on Earth, here and now.

One of the most poetic definitions of Feng Shui comes from author and thinker, Stephen Feuchtwan:

"Knowing how to choose the correct place, at the perfect moment; the correct alignment with the directions of the Universe, combined with the efficient use of objects with mystical reverence, is harmony...is peace...is Feng Shui."

The Schools of Feng Shui

The two main schools of Feng Shui are:

1. Form School
2. Compass School

Each school has different names used to designate it.

Form School (Hsing-Shih) is also known as the School of Configurations, The Kanchow Method, and the Kiangsi Method.

Compass School is also known as the School of Directions and Positions (Fang-Wei) and as the Method of Men, the Method of House and Homes and the Fukien School.

It is not important which school of Feng Shui is studied and used, both are based on the universal principles of harmony. The main objective of Feng Shui is to harmonize our surroundings with the universal creative force known as Chi.

Each year is made up of twelve months and during every month there are moments in which the force of Chi is vigorous and other times when this force is weaker. It is akin to human breathing. Knowledge of the rhythms and the polarities of the forces of Yin and Yang is fundamental in creating harmonious surroundings.

Feng Shui: The Harmony of Life

The relationship between man and his home is intimate and subtle. When we arrive home and feel good, it is because the surroundings are healthy and balanced. There is something invisible that cannot be perceived through the senses, but is felt. That something is the spirit of the place. Through Feng Shui, the spirit of the space speaks to us in a language of light and shapes, making us aware of the patterns that we ourselves have created in our homes, the places we work and in our own lives.

Feng Shui is based on observing nature and how it manifests its vitality, beauty, harmony and peace.

Over the centuries, the philosophy of Feng Shui has been influenced by different cultures. Master Lin Yun details the process as follows:

1. The millennia-old tradition of Tibet (Bon) - First Level
2. The Hindu-Buddhist culture - Second Level
3. The Chinese-Confucius culture - Third Level
4. The culture of the modern world - Fourth Level

Feng Shui contains knowledge that comes from the traditions of Buddhism, the Tao, The Book of Changes - the I-Ching and from Chinese astrology.

As mentioned before, there are two methods or principle schools of Feng Shui: 1) Compass School and 2) Form School.

Compass School uses analytical methods and a compass to find the alignment of buildings and spaces, based on the cardinal points, to establish the relationships between them.

Form School uses transcendental methods and establishes relationships based on the natural shapes of the space. The essence of this method is based on the placement of the entrance of vital life-force, or the Mouth of Chi, of the building or space and the subsequent use of the lines of harmony or energy fields.

This book of Feng Shui follows the Form School philosophy as taught by Master Thomas Lin Yun, the highest authority of the Fourth Level of Feng Shui.

The Fourth Level of Feng Shui is the integration of the tradition of Form School with modern science. Among the scientific disciplines that have influenced Feng Shui are Bioenergetics, Ergonomics, Architecture, Environmental Engineering and especially Biological Construction or Bau-Biologie. The science of Bau-Biologie is the study and design of harmonious living environments using materials and shapes to help maintain energy efficiency and the health of those who live or work there. Many Feng Shui practitioners are "Bau-biologists." The director of the International Institute of Bau-Biologie is architect and builder, Reinhard Konuka. Although German by birth, Mr. Konuka has his research and design center in New Zealand. There is an office of the International Institute of Bau-Biologie in the United States. If you are interested in studying Bau-Biologie you can contact:

> The Institute of Bau-Biologie
> PO Box 387
> Clearwater, FL 34615
> Tel: 813-461-4371

> *There are three things that govern our lives.*
> *The first is destiny, the second is luck,*
> *the third is Feng Shui.*

II

FENG SHUI IN PRACTICE

住家的傳統風水解法

雲石居士林石敬題

一九七七七日於香港

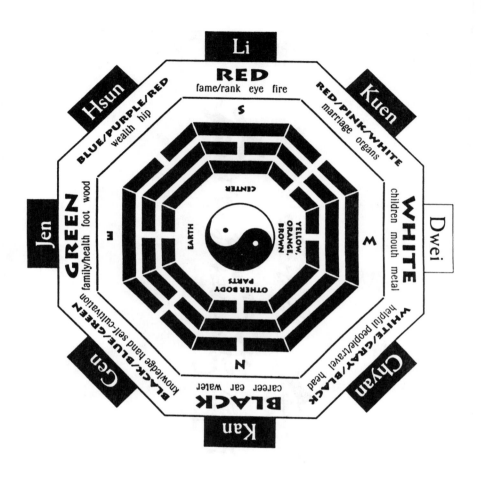

The Ba-Gua with Some of its Correspondences

How Feng Shui is Used

The student should become familiarized with the philosophy of Feng Shui, its theories and methods of observation: visible and invisible. After having located the problems within the space being studied, solutions to these problems can be carried out. These can be visible solutions or invisible solutions (also called transcendental).

The practical application of Feng Shui can be delineated in two phases and methods of solutions.

OBSERVATIONS	
VISIBLE Yang	INVISIBLE Yin
SOLUTIONS	
TANGIBLE Yang	TRANSCENDENTAL Yin
OBJECT	

Visible Observations

Visible observations are those we can perceive through our five senses. Among them are observing the neighborhood, the vegetation that surrounds the area, the elevation of the land and the presence of any hills, mountains or valleys. If the vegetation is poor, this generally indicates poor Chi; while if there is abundant and green vegetation with lush trees, this is an indication of prosperous Chi. We must also look at what else is in the area: other buildings, roads and highways, railroads, airports, telephone and electrical poles, transformers, bridges, rivers, lakes and oceans. The shape of the land and the house, the layout of the rooms, the location of the bathrooms and kitchen, the placement of the furniture and the colors used must all be considered. The shapes of the design elements: walls, columns, beams and doors are also important factors to consider. Visible observations include using the lines of harmony, or Ba-Gua, to find out how the shape of the house and its rooms are affecting the quality of life, based on the flow of Chi.

FENG SHUI: THE HARMONY OF LIFE

OBSERVATIONS AND SOLUTIONS

OBSERVATIONS

VISIBLE

INVISIBLE

External Factors:
Chi of the land
Placement of the habitat
Technological influences
Shape of the land
Shape of the house
Other factors

External Factors:
History of the neighborhood
Chi of the neighborhood
Other factors

Internal Factors:
Design of the home
Layout of the home
Doors and windows
Stairs
Kitchen and bathrooms
Placement of furniture
Other factors

Internal Factors:
History of the home
Chi of the home
Other factors

SOLUTIONS

VISIBLE OR MUNDANE

INVISIBLE OR TRANSCENDENTAL

Traditional
Nine Minor Additions
Other solutions

Three Secrets
Tracing the Nine Stars
Other solutions

The word Ba-Gua means «eight symbols that hang up there.» It is a traditional Chinese symbol in the shape of an octagon. Each side corresponds to a trigram and a number of correspondences that can be understood on different levels. For example, each line of the Ba-Gua is associated with an everyday activity or life area. This is the principle that we use in Feng Shui to establish the intimate relationship between man and the buildings he inhabits.

Visualizing the lines of harmony of the Ba-Gua around the perimeter of the land and house is the first step in knowing if the layout is suitable. To do this, we divide each side of the house in three equal parts that then lets us overlay the octagon. Areas that are cut out or missing within the octagon weaken the Chi of the space, while areas that extend past or are additions to the main area strengthen Chi. By overlaying the Ba-Gua on the space, we can locate the areas that correspond to the main activities of the people who live there. Inside, each room also has its own individual Ba-Gua.

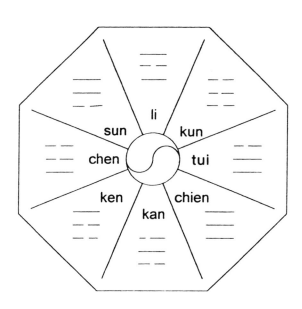

The Ba-Gua

When visualizing or mentally drawing the Ba-Gua around the perimeter of the house, we must always line the main entrance up with the line of water (knowledge, career and benefactors). The area to the left (looking straight ahead) corresponds to self-cultivation, learning or knowledge. Toward the center of this line is the energy that corresponds to our lives' mission, career and our professional life. To the right is the benefactors area and is related to our father both physical and spiritual, to what we expect and hope from others and to what we desire from our friendships.

The following diagram shows the layout of the eight life areas around the home. The correct shape of the lines of harmony is an octagon, but in this example a rectangle is used to help you visualize it. When the Ba-Gua is used this way, the elements, colors and life activities are laid out in the proper manner. The total number of life activities is nine: eight trigrams that form the lines of the octagon and its center which symbolizes the harmonious union of the other eight forces.

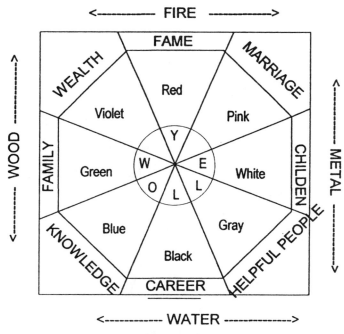

The main entrance - the Mouth of Chi

The Lines of Harmony of the Ba-Gua

VIOLET	FIRE-RED	PINK

WOOD-GREEN

FINANCES	FAME	MARRIAGE
FAMILY	HEALTH	CHILDREN
KNOWLEDGE	PROFESSION	BENEFACTORS

METAL-WHITE

← ALIGN WITH THE MAIN ENTRANCE →

BLUE	WATER-BLACK	GRAY

The left wall represents wood, is associated with the color green in the area of family, and is connected with our past, our grandparents and ancestors. It is feminine in character.

The wall to the right represents metal, is associated with the color white in the children area, and is connected with the fruit of our lives, our children and our creativity. It is masculine in character.

The front wall of the home is Yang in nature and masculine.

The far wall is Yin in nature and feminine in character.

Invisible Observations

Invisible or intangible observations are those we are unable to detect through our five senses. They may be manifest or transcendental in nature. Manifested observations are those that can be perceived with the use of instruments that detect the presence of electromagnetic energy (radio waves, radar, micro-waves, infrared rays, ultraviolet waves, X-rays, gamma rays, beta rays and cosmic rays, among others) and other instruments such as pendulums, dowsing rods, and others that help us perceive geomagnetic and cosmic energies that are present in our surroundings. Transcendental manifestations include the history of the place, the quality of life in the neighborhood as well as the history and spirit of the location. These invisible factors have a notable influence. Perceiving these different energies and knowing the history of the location tells us about the quality of the environment which directly affects the quality of life.

Once we have identified the existing problems, we will apply the appropriate Feng Shui decorating solutions to create a harmonious environment.

Visible Solutions

Visible solutions come from Feng Shui tradition. They are the principles of the tradition for homes and businesses as well as the Nine Minor Additions.

Some principles of the tradition for homes and businesses are covered later.

The Nine Minor Additions are a series of decorative objects. Choosing a particular Addition depends on what our intuition tells us. When a space needs to be adjusted, any of the Nine Minor Additions will work.

For example, if we need to reinforce the area of our life related to career or profession; perhaps we are looking for a job, want to change our place of employment or want a promotion in our current job, we should place a light or bright object in the career area (located in the center of the front wall where the front entrance is located).

As we have seen in the diagram on the previous page, career or profession vibrates with the water element. So, placing a water fountain in the career area will also activate Chi here. Placing flags, pictures or illustrations of water scenes will also honor the water element.

Although the Minor Additions are visible solutions, there are also a number of them that are transcendental in nature including mirrors, Ba-Guas and Chinese bamboo flutes.

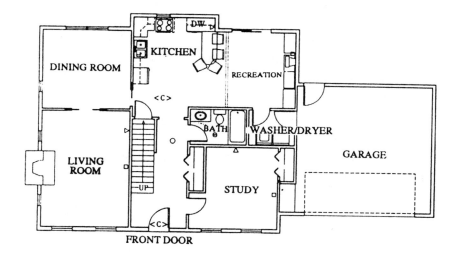

Situations that need adjustment:
1) Kitchen facing the front door
2) Biting staircase
3) Bathroom in the health area (center)

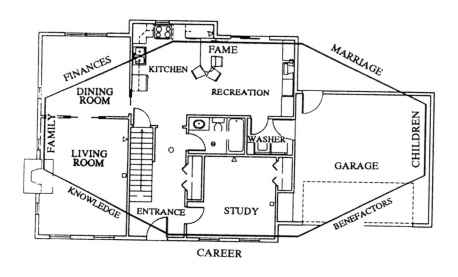

Using the Ba-Gua on a Home's Floor Plan

Invisible or Transcendental Solutions

Among the invisible and transcendental solutions are: The Three Secrets, Tracing the Nine Stars, the Transcendental Uses of the Ba-Gua and Sealing the Doors.

Examples of the Ancient Art of Feng Shui

It is interesting to learn that the areas of the home are related to different activities in our lives be it personal relationships, marriage, finances, physical and mental health, career or profession. Knowing where each of these activities lie within a home allows us to honor them, which affects that particular area of our lives.

In Feng Shui, decorative objects are always placed in the appropriate location. If we want to reinforce our family's financial situation, we can place appropriate objects in the finances area. If we want to activate personal relationships or marriage, we would put decorative objects in that area the corresponds to marriage.

Several Miami businesses have been noticeably helped by hanging crystals or placing lights in the front entrance of their businesses. Feng Shui crystal balls are made of Austrian crystal that have multiple facets and a small hole at the top to hang a cord through. They vary in size from 20 mm to 100 mm. The crystal balls are hung 9 inches from the ceiling (or 9 cm, the important point is that the distance is in units of nine). When the front door of a business is in the area of benefactors, installing a light with two bulbs is also good. It should be installed with the light shining inward to reinforce the energy related with increasing clientele.

Reinforcing the energy in the children area has lead to successful pregnancies in a number of families who have wanted children. This area can be adjusted with wind chimes and plants with white flowers. By using white, which corresponds to this area, we are reinforcing the energy associated with children, our live's creation. Installing lights, especially if this area is missing in the layout or is dark, is also appropriate. In these cases, it is also a good idea to reinforce these adjustments with the Three Secrets, a transcendental solution (See page 114).

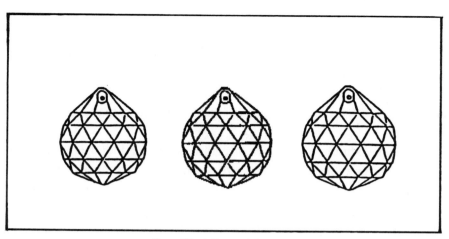

Feng Shui Crystal Balls

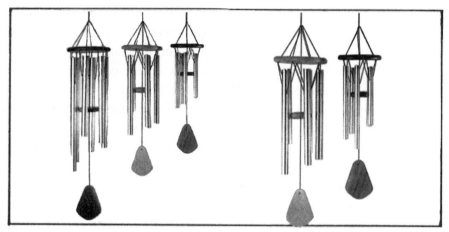

One of our Feng Shui students was having economic trouble. He owned a business and was having a difficult time collecting past-due balances. Often problems that show up in a business originate in the home. After examining his house, I saw that his bed was located in the middle of the room and in direct line with the door; in essence, his bed was adrift. I suggested a number of different alternatives for positioning his bed. The head of the bed should always be up against a solid wall. This position fortifies Chi and provides a sense of security that is then reflected in that person's day-to-day life. The direction the bed faces, with respect to the Ba-Gua, determines which of the life activities will be reinforced. For this man, we chose to locate it in the area of finances. A few days after changing the position of his bed, collections and sales in his business increased measurably.

If we would like to receive help in our personal relationships, we would put the head of the bed in the marriage area. If we wish to strengthen our goals, plans or projects, we would position it in the fame area. If we would like to receive help with finances, the head of the bed should be in the finances area, and so on.

The bed should never be in direct line with the door used to enter the room. Sleeping with your head toward a window also weakens Chi, but not as much as having it aligned with the door. The Feng Shui solution to having the head of the bed against a window is to hang a crystal ball from the window pane. When the bed is in line with the door, if it is not possible to reposition the bed, a crystal ball should be hung between the entrance door and the bed.

A chiropractor didn't have sufficient capital to buy the new machines he needed for his practice. I suggested, among other things, that he hang a Feng Shui crystal ball on a red cord, 9 inches from the ceiling, and place a small lamp with a purple light bulb in the finances area. These changes were then reinforced with the Three Secrets. A few days later, he received money from some outstanding bills and he sold an apartment that he had had on the market for a long time. His finances had indeed begun to improve.

Hanging crystals -according to their shape and colors- in the appropriate areas of the Ba-Gua has surprising effects on people's lives. Color transcends shape and shape transcends material. Crystals correspond to the water element, but what activates the element or energy that we wish to mobilize is our intention. A crystal pyramid represents the fire element if we activate its pyramid shape with the Three Secrets; pyramid or cone shapes correspond to the fire element. When a cone shaped object -be it wood, metal, or crystal- has its shape activated, it represents the fire element and should be placed in the corresponding area of the Ba-Gua. It should then be reinforced with the Three Secrets. Then, we can watch to see the changes that manifest in our lives in respect to reaching our goals, our ideals or fame -which are activated by the fire element.

An astrologer in Miami placed crystals in areas corresponding to the lines of harmony of the Ba-Gua: an amethyst (purple) in the finances area, a red quartz pyramid in the fame area, a rose quartz in the marriage area, and

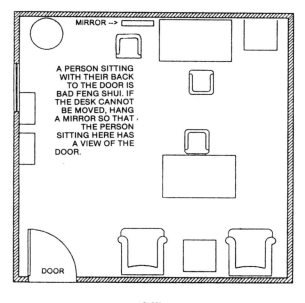

MIRROR -->

A PERSON SITTING
WITH THEIR BACK
TO THE DOOR IS
BAD FENG SHUI. IF
THE DESK CANNOT
BE MOVED, HANG
A MIRROR SO THAT
THE PERSON
SITTING HERE HAS
A VIEW OF THE
DOOR.

DOOR

Office

onyx streaked with white in the area of benefactors. These changes were reinforced with the Three Secrets. The results were very good. His income increased considerably, enough so that he could afford a new house.

In Form School, the front entrance represents where energy or Chi enters. Life manifests through water. The line of water is always a continuation of the Mouth of Chi, which is the principle entrance or the front door of the house. The area in front of the door should always be clear. Any plants with thorns, representing the cone shape of the fire element, will produce aggressive and conflictive energy. Thorny plants should be placed on the patio or behind the house. There shouldn't be any plants or flowers in the front of the house with thorns.

The front door is very important. Double doors are the most favorable. The path that leads up to the front door should be the same width or larger than the door itself. Chi is weakened when it encounters straight and narrow paths, so we should have a curved path or another alternative that reinforces Chi. If the path leading to the door is straight, some Feng Shui solutions would be to hang flags, place a water fountain, plants, lights or other objects that give

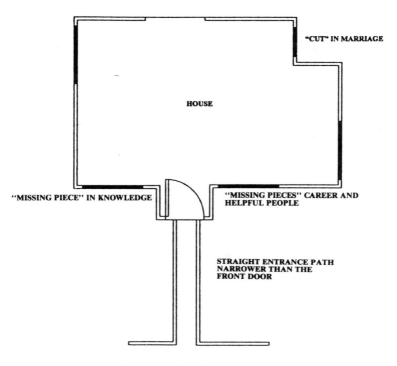

SLIDING GLASS DOORS
ALIGNED WITH THE
FRONT DOOR

"CUT" IN MARRIAGE

HOUSE

"MISSING PIECE" IN KNOWLEDGE

"MISSING PIECES" CAREER AND
HELPFUL PEOPLE

STRAIGHT ENTRANCE PATH
NARROWER THAN THE
FRONT DOOR

Bad Feng Shui

the impression of expansion. Two lights placed on either side of a narrow path increase visibility and open it up to receive Chi.

When the front door is aligned with sliding glass doors that face the back patio, a vacuum effect is produced inside the house which drains Chi. This is true even more so when there is a pool or lush trees beyond the sliding doors, as Chi enters and leaves quickly creating a void. The energy that escapes affects the different life activities of the family. Personal relationships or those with children will be weakened in this situation by the pulling effect the wood element of the trees and the water element of the pool have on the home's Chi. In cases like this, the energy inside should be balanced with the energy outside to create harmony. Live plants can be placed inside the house on either side of the sliding glass doors. Crystal balls can also be placed in the center panels of the doors. Hang wind chimes, pictures with views of nature, green landscapes and forests.

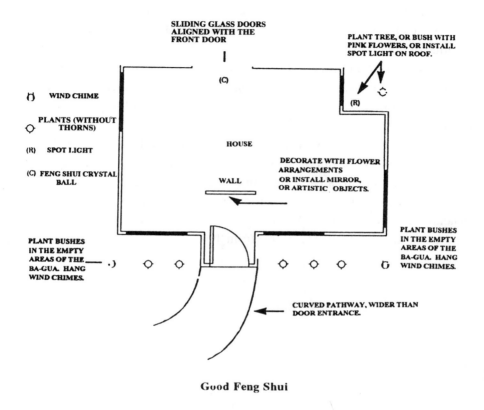

SLIDING GLASS DOORS ALIGNED WITH THE FRONT DOOR

PLANT TREE, OR BUSH WITH PINK FLOWERS, OR INSTALL SPOT LIGHT ON ROOF.

(C)

(R)

WIND CHIME

PLANTS (WITHOUT THORNS)

(R)   SPOT LIGHT

(C) FENG SHUI CRYSTAL BALL

HOUSE

WALL

DECORATE WITH FLOWER ARRANGEMENTS OR INSTALL MIRROR, OR ARTISTIC OBJECTS.

PLANT BUSHES IN THE EMPTY AREAS OF THE BA-GUA. HANG WIND CHIMES.

PLANT BUSHES IN THE EMPTY AREAS OF THE BA-GUA. HANG WIND CHIMES.

CURVED PATHWAY, WIDER THAN DOOR ENTRANCE.

Good Feng Shui

We have seen many businesses and homes that lack the vital life force of plants. Some people think that plants produce allergens and increase humidity and so prefer to use artificial ones. In Feng Shui, we can use artificial plants if their texture and color are of high quality. However, often live plants are needed.

Live plants not only bring vital life force into a space, they also purify it which helps to counteract the effects of many toxic substances and products that are frequently present in our homes and offices. Air can be purified by two distinct methods, one of which is to use an air purifier. These appliances usually use an activated carbon filter that traps impurities and toxic out-gases like formaldehyde (which is generally given off by synthetic carpets). How well these purifiers work depends on their size and quality. They tend to work well as long as the filters are changed frequently. The other method of purifying the air is by using live plants. During the day, plants generate oxygen as they cleanse the air of carbon dioxide and other toxic substances. NASA was one of the first U.S. governmental organizations to investigate this use; they used plants to eliminate toxic substances from the air in the space shuttles. These studies showed that plants are more effective than mechanical filters for controlling toxic substances like benzene, trichloroethylene and formaldehyde.

Live plants improve the quality of the air we breathe. But it isn't necessary to live in the middle of a jungle, a medium sized plant cleans the air in a ten-meter square area. Plants in homes and offices also increase the humidity which compensates for the excessive dryness that air conditioners or heating systems produce. Among the plants that are recommended for Feng Shui are: arum, palms, yucca, plants from the diffenbachia family and pothos dorados.

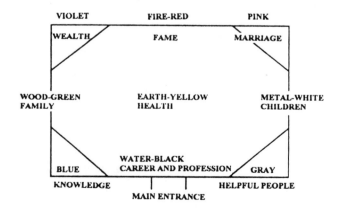

**The Line of Water Represents where
Energy Enters and Life Manifests**

I did another Feng Shui consultation on a restaurant on the beach. The previous owners had kept the business only under much duress. As I mentioned, one of the principles of Feng Shui is to know the history of the place, which in this case was not favorable. None of the previous businesses had had success in this locale. The decoration consisted of a series of pictures hung on the wall which showed a line of colored fish swimming in the ocean. It appeared to be a caravan of fish headed out the door of the business. The message of the pictures was clear: «Let's all get out of here!» This type of message is very subtle but effective. The rest of the decorations produced similar effects. The shelves at the entrance were heavy and aggressive, both blocking and repelling energy from coming in. The bathrooms had been built in the finances and fame areas. The space corresponding to the rest of the fame area as well as the relationship area was occupied by a large freezer. The entrance door was narrow and aligned with closed off areas. In general, the space was very unbalanced. These are the recommendations that we made for the new owner:

1) Hang mirrors on the outside of the bathroom doors to eliminate their conflictive effect on the finances and fame areas. Paint the bathrooms: the men's room in the finances area should be purple, and the women's in the fame area should be light pink. Place the stereo system in the finances area as reinforcement -its electromagnetic energy activates finances.
2) Reorient the fish pictures so that they would appear to be swimming into the restaurant.
3) Install mirrors on the sides facing the front door to give the impression of more space which increases the energy that enters through the door.
4) Place a circular rug in the entrance to welcome clients.
5) Install a lamp with two lights and a Feng Shui crystal ball in the main entrance to encourage Chi to enter.
6) Install a water fountain with falling water inside the restaurant in the benefactors area.
7) Hang plants from the ceiling so their color and beauty could purify and harmonize the space.
8) Other changes: Colors for the walls, decoration for each area of the Ba-Gua, music, table placement, and location of the signs.

A friend of the family came to us with a financial problem. We suggested that she put a fish tank in the benefactors area. She followed our advice and a week later, received offers from a number of clients who were interested in her works of art. She began selling her art which quickly improved her financial situation.

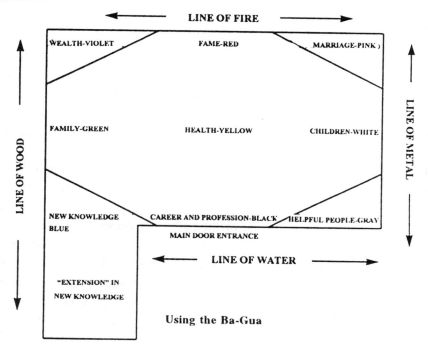

Using the Ba-Gua

A flower shop in Boca Raton, Florida had a history of ups and downs in their business. Recently, the situation had gotten worse when another florist opened up shop in the same area. After examining the business, we made a few recommendations to the owner. One of the problems was the back door. The back area, that of finances, fame and relationships was affected by an alley that ran behind the business which was used for delivery trucks and garbage collection. Some of our suggestions included installing a mirror underneath the cash register and placing live plants near it, hanging coins from the ten Chinese emperors and scattering bird seed in the alley. When birds fly, they move their wings bringing happiness and an influx of Chi. A few days later, after having made these changes, business began to improve and sales went up.

A doctor asked for our advice to improve relations between the employees in his office. The problems stemmed from personality clashes, but the doctor wanted to do everything in his power to hold on to all his employees. We suggested that he hang a number of bells and wind chimes in the hallways and the conference room. Almost all of the desks were up against the wall. We suggested he install mirrors so that the employees had more visibility of what was going on behind them. Placing plants and hanging pictures with nature scenes helped create a more harmonious space. The music system was broken, so we advised him to get is fixed and to play soft, classical music. These changes had amazing effects; employee relations improved quickly once these and other adjustments were in place.

When business is slow, burn some incense and wave it over the telephone, cash register, credit card machine and the person behind the counter. Reinforce it with the Three Secrets.

The best position for metal furniture, accessories and equipment is in the children area of the Ba-Gua. This activates creativity and improves relations between parents and children. Reinforce any adjustments made with the Three Secrets.

It is best that the proportion of windows to doors in a home is no more than 3:1.

Increase your income and your financial situation by installing a fish tank in the finances area of your home, office or business whether that be the living room or any other room. The aquarium symbolizes the flow of money and prosperity.

Plant leafy trees on the left side of the house (as you face it). The trees should not be in line with, or too close to, windows or doors. The left side of the home corresponds to the wood element. Trees act as barriers that protect and nurture the area around them with their vital life energy.

Chi becomes stagnant and does not flow when rooms, wardrobes or drawers are full of dusty objects that are never used. Get organized and select only those objects that you really need and want. Do away with the rest; sell them or give them away. As you begin getting rid of objects in your space, you are also cleaning away ties to the past that keep you from developing and evolving. The empty space that remains will attract positive energy, vitality and prosperity.

The flow of Chi meets resistance with spiral staircases, stairs that face or are biting a door to the street, floors of differing levels, slanted walls and ceilings, walls that bite or block an entrance door, dead-end hallways, dark corners, stairway landings and cramped spaces (like under stairways). Solutions: Hang wind chimes, crystal balls, place plants in the corners and on stairway landings, use floral arrangements, hang Chinese bamboo flutes, among other possibilities. Reinforce with the Three Secrets.

When you notice that things aren't going so well, that you are having difficulty at work and your wishes, being in your best interest and without selfish motives, are not being fulfilled, mediate about your home. Think about the shapes, the furniture, the colors and objects in your space, what they are like and where they are located. Think of how you might better place them so that each area in your home is more harmonious. After careful observation and analysis, begin applying Feng Shui principles to your space. For example, hang the appropriate colored wallpaper in the bathroom located in the finances area, paint each room its corresponding color, hang mirrors or crystal balls in the appropriate spaces, hang wind chimes or Chinese flutes to elevate and reinforce Chi. Feng Shui is a way to change patterns that restrict and block prosperity, happiness, physical abundance and harmony. Change what is most urgent in your life now and watch to see how new solutions emerge. Take it step by step.

If your relationship with your partner is stressed, quietly go out and buy a small plant with pink flowers and place it in the relationship area of the bedroom. Reinforce it with the Three Secrets. To keep the harmony, do this each week.

A space's Chi should complement the personal Chi of those who live or work there so that harmony is created in all its aspects, mundane as well as spiritual.

Rooms that are dark and narrow have a lot of Yin energy and should be decorated with mirrors, lights, pictures of landscapes and expansive views -all Yang attributes, to create a more harmonious space.

Rooms that are very spacious and light have an excess of Yang energy and should be decorated with plants, heavy pieces of art, sculptures, furniture, rugs with circular shapes and dark colors -all Yin attributes.

All Feng Shui decorations should be reinforced with the Three Secrets.

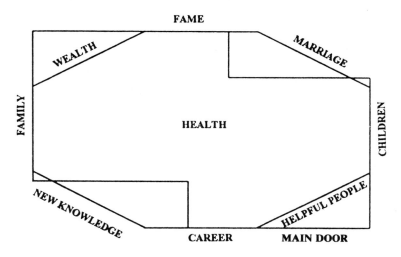

Life Areas that are Affected: 1) Marriage 2) Knowledge

Urban Feng Shui

The center of Feng Shui is found in Hong Kong, the most sophisticated city in the Far East. Hong Kong is home to many multinational companies that compete in both markets, East and West. There is no other city in the Far East that uses Feng Shui more than Hong Kong. The majority of businesses and families with economic clout consult Feng Shui experts before buying land or beginning construction on their homes or buildings. A real estate advertisement speaks of a luxurious apartment with wonderful amenities and an excellent view of the South China Sea. In addition, it mentions of the quality of Feng Shui present in the design and the shape of the building. The Chinese emperors always consulted with Feng Shui experts before choosing the site and designs for their palaces and monuments.

Even when a city has good urban planning, new buildings can change it. Residential neighborhoods that have plenty of green areas, walkways, parks, lakes and good Chi are often changed with the construction of apartment buildings, corners, highways and other buildings that destroy the harmony of what was there originally.

In cities, buildings take the place of hills and mountains, the streets are the rivers and vegetation is the vital life-force. The shapes of the buildings,

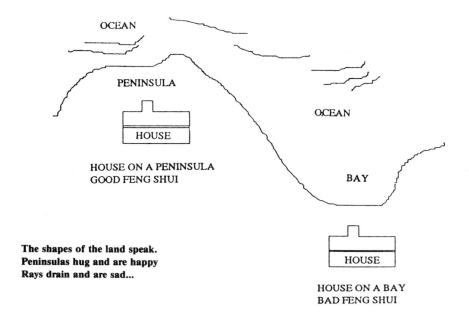

OCEAN

PENINSULA

HOUSE

HOUSE ON A PENINSULA
GOOD FENG SHUI

OCEAN

BAY

HOUSE

HOUSE ON A BAY
BAD FENG SHUI

**The shapes of the land speak.
Peninsulas hug and are happy
Rays drain and are sad...**

the alignment of streets and the presence of vegetation are very important factors that affect the harmony of a community.

Frequently new buildings alter the Chi of a locale. A family came to us for help when a new apartment building's construction overshadowed and pressed in on their apartment. One of the traditional solutions is to hang hexagonal mirrors on the outside of the house to reflect and return any type of negative influence. Ba-Gua mirrors can also be used. There are three types: flat, concave and convex. A convex mirror reduces adverse or negative influences that come from outside. It should not be used in the entrance of a business as it could reduce the number of clients who enter. (Though this negative effect can be solved by using the Three Secrets.) A concave mirror attracts and retains energy where it is being siphoned off as with rivers and streets that flow away from the building.

A famous real estate investor, Donald Trump, decided to use a Feng Shui expert to change the design of a number of his buildings. The results were so positive that he has continued to use Feng Shui on all his properties ever since. There are many cases like this in the U.S.

In 1990, another real estate developer built an office tower in Coconut Grove, Florida. A few weeks after finishing construction, the most important tenant declared bankruptcy, leaving the building virtually empty. One of the principle stock holders deemed the situation «chaotic.» Among the partners in the real estate company was a Chinese man. He suggested bringing in a Feng Shui Master from China to go over the building's design. By 1993, half of the building was still not leased. Finally, they decided to bring in a Feng Shui Master who immediately told them that the building's design impeded the flow of Chi. The main entrance was blocked by a water fountain and a sculpture that had very sharp and aggressive angles. The lobby design also blocked and restricted the flow of energy. The Feng Shui Master went through the entire building and recommended changes in the design of the main entrance and the manager's office. Not long after making these adjustments, the building's luck began to change. New businesses began signing leasing contracts and a number of already existing tenants expanded their businesses. Now this office tower has 100% occupancy. This developer is now building an apartment complex in that same area using the principles of Feng Shui. The building has a majestic view of the ocean and its lines and balconies have pleasing shapes without sharp corners or missing pieces.

Feng Shui is a tool capable of creating harmony in buildings, spaces and people themselves. The nature of this art can also be seen in the ancient Greek. Roman and Arabic cultures. However, this ancient tool is something very new for our modern architecture and culture. It is a system that helps to open up our awareness and integrate it with nature. And its arrival in the West comes none too soon, as we find ourselves overwhelmed by a multitude of problems. The destruction of our ecological system is affecting the very basis of life on the planet. The ancient method of Feng Shui, with its logical and illogical solutions, teaches us to create harmonious spaces. With it, we have the opportunity to complement our modern culture (Yang) with the simplicity of solutions that come to us from long ago (Yin) to create the unity of Tao.

Solutions from the Tradition for Homes and Offices

During times of change and periods of much work and stress, simple adjustments, based on the tradition of Feng Shui, can be of great help. They can bring more clarity of thought, mental well being and prosperity. The following are nine ways to improve a space:

1. For more clarity, hang a bronze wind chime exactly nine units (9 inches, 27 cm, etc...) from the ceiling inside the front door.
2. For help with intellectual matters, place books in view of the front door.
3. For better mental and physical health, position both your bed and desk so that you have a view of the door.
4. For stress reduction, hang two mirrors facing each other so that when you enter your home or office, you have to pass between them.
5. To cultivate love, harmony and understanding with your partner, hang a circular mirror in the bedroom.
6. To improve your financial situation, install a mirror in the kitchen behind the stove so that the burners are reflected in it. Burners represent wealth and good luck.
7. To improve the general well being of a space, place flowers in the bedroom, study and kitchen.
8. To reinforce personal evolution, move 27 objects that have not been moved in the past year.
9. During difficult times, do breathing exercises with the light of the moon.

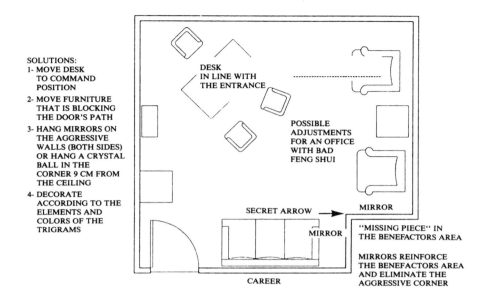

SOLUTIONS:
1- MOVE DESK TO COMMAND POSITION
2- MOVE FURNITURE THAT IS BLOCKING THE DOOR'S PATH
3- HANG MIRRORS ON THE AGGRESSIVE WALLS (BOTH SIDES) OR HANG A CRYSTAL BALL IN THE CORNER 9 CM FROM THE CEILING
4- DECORATE ACCORDING TO THE ELEMENTS AND COLORS OF THE TRIGRAMS

DESK IN LINE WITH THE ENTRANCE

POSSIBLE ADJUSTMENTS FOR AN OFFICE WITH BAD FENG SHUI

SECRET ARROW

MIRROR

MIRROR

"MISSING PIECE" IN THE BENEFACTORS AREA

MIRRORS REINFORCE THE BENEFACTORS AREA AND ELIMINATE THE AGGRESSIVE CORNER

CAREER

Principles of the Tradition for Businesses

Every business that is growing requires constant attention to the sales, administration, finances and creative effort of all those involved. By using the Chinese art of Feng Shui, owners and employees alike can make simple, inexpensive changes that generate better cooperation and more success for the business. The following are a few simple ways to create an atmosphere of prosperity and growth:

For expanding vision and imagination, place a small circular mirror under your pillow.

For stimulating your creative spirit, place a small brass bell in the center of the right-hand side of your desk.

For reinforcing your vision and mental clarity, use a spacious desk that has enough space for the expansion of your ideas.

For helping you make correct decisions, place your desk in the power position -the left-hand corner of the wall that is farthest from the main entrance of the office.

For increasing your efficiency and your personal magnetism, position your desk so you have a view of the entrance door, but are not directly in line

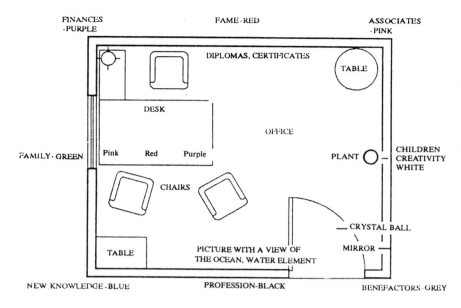

FINANCES -PURPLE   FAME - RED   ASSOCIATES - PINK

DIPLOMAS, CERTIFICATES

TABLE

DESK

OFFICE

FAMILY - GREEN   Pink   Red   Purple   PLANT   CHILDREN CREATIVITY WHITE

CHAIRS

CRYSTAL BALL

TABLE   PICTURE WITH A VIEW OF THE OCEAN, WATER ELEMENT   MIRROR

NEW KNOWLEDGE - BLUE   PROFESSION - BLACK   BENEFACTORS - GREY

MOVE THE DESK TO THE POWER
POSITION (IF POSSIBLE)

BAD FENG SHUI
1 - DESK IN FRONT
OF THE DOOR
2 - DOOR THAT OPENS
THE WRONG WAY

SOLUTIONS:
1 - HANG A FENG SHUI CRYSTAL BALL
BETWEEN THE DESK AND DOOR
2 - HANG A MIRROR IN THE ENTRANCE
3 - HONOR THE COLORS OF THE TRIGRAMS
-FINANCES -FAME AND RELATIONSHIPS
(COLORS, PICTURES, LAMPS, LIVE
PLANTS)
4 - HONOR COLORS ON THE DESK
OTHERS-

with it. Place your back against a solid wall, which is much better than a window.

For mental clarity and concentration, hang a wind chime above the right side of your desk.

To give more credence to your point of view, hang a small bell on a red string on the inside handle of your office door.

For activating your creativity, hang two mirrors on either side of your desk.

For clear thinking and effective negotiations with difficult people, sit in a chair with a high back, have a solid wall behind you and a view of the entrance door from where you are sitting.

For reinforcing the image, fame and reputation of the company, place red flowers in the center of the wall opposite the front door of the office.

For expanding the goals of the company, hang a wind chime in the center of the conference room.

For increasing the spirit of cooperation among employees, light the hallways well, especially if there are many doors.

For rallying public support, visualize the faces of 5 people who can help your business. Do this at least 3 times a day during 3 or 9 days.

For good sales figures, get rid of anything that may be blocking doors, both at the office and at home.

For increasing your market, when you are alone, scatter bird seed from the front door onto the sidewalk.

For good luck, choose a business locale where the previous tenants were successful.

For increasing efficiency and productivity, the bathroom doors should not be visible from the main entrance.

For improving the business' finances, collect water from nine prosperous businesses, place it in a container and put it in the left-hand corner of the wall farthest from the main entrance.

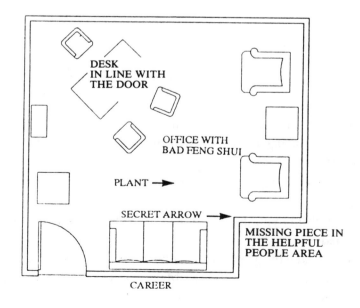

DESK
IN LINE WITH
THE DOOR

OFFICE WITH
BAD FENG SHUI

PLANT →

SECRET ARROW →

MISSING PIECE IN
THE HELPFUL
PEOPLE AREA

CAREER

If you work with angular shapes that point at you (such as where two walls jut out and meet or square columns) move your desk or soften the corners with plants, a wind chime, or a Feng Shui crystal ball. The ball should be 20 mm in diameter and be hung nine units (inches or centimeters) from the ceiling in line with the sharp edge.

For increasing profits, hang a mirror where it reflects water, which is a symbol of wealth.

For improving sales, make the sales people work as close to the main door as possible.

For moving large quantities of merchandise, chose a locale that has a large door.

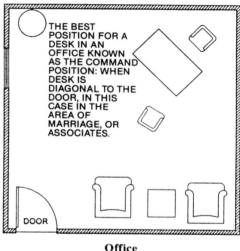

THE BEST POSITION FOR A DESK IN AN OFFICE KNOWN AS THE COMMAND POSITION: WHEN DESK IS DIAGONAL TO THE DOOR, IN THIS CASE IN THE AREA OF MARRIAGE, OR ASSOCIATES.

DOOR

Office

To cultivate prosperity and harmony in your business, place fresh flowers in the manager's office, in the reception area and in the employees' break room.

To make your employees work better, avoid placing their desks in line with the door.

To multiply your fame and success, hang a wind chime over the head of your bed.

To quicken the growth of your business, say hello to nine new people every day for 27 consecutive days. Make sure that you do it with happiness and without adding any negative comments.

The main door to the business is the one the was built initially. When another door takes its place as the entrance, the energy of the business always suffers -usually a loss of opportunity.

The lid to the toilet should always be put down after flushing and should remain so between uses. This prevents luck and prosperity from being flushed from the business (or home).

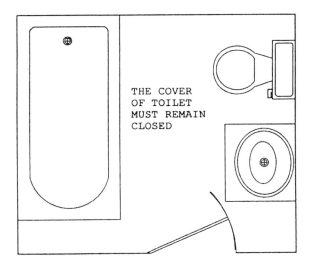

THE COVER
OF TOILET
MUST REMAIN
CLOSED

The business' cash register should be located in the finances area. If this isn't feasible, then it should be put as close to the front door as possible. The finances area should be reinforced with a light, lamp or a television if the cash register can't be placed there.

If the cash register is placed in the knowledge area, success will depend on the work and dedication of the owner. The benefactors area is much better for attracting success as it facilitates unexpected help and popularity.

To increase vital life-force, hang a Chinese bamboo flute over the inside door frame of your office.

Two lights installed in the benefactors area will attract clients and popularity.

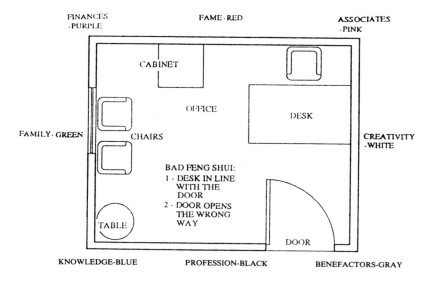

FINANCES -PURPLE   FAME - RED   ASSOCIATES -PINK

CABINET

OFFICE

DESK

FAMILY - GREEN

CHAIRS

CREATIVITY -WHITE

BAD FENG SHUI:
1 - DESK IN LINE WITH THE DOOR
2 - DOOR OPENS THE WRONG WAY

TABLE

DOOR

KNOWLEDGE-BLUE   PROFESSION-BLACK   BENEFACTORS-GRAY

The surface of ceilings, walls and floors should be smooth. Chi does not flow properly when the floor has different levels.

Before moving, find out about the background of the locale. If the previous business was successful, it means there is positive Chi for that type of business.

When looking for a new locale, keep foot and car traffic in mind. It is important to check if there is easy access to the entrance of the building or commercial center. The example on the next page shows some businesses. Locales 1 and 2 are well positioned, though 3 is the best as its main door is wide with good visibility. Establishment 4 has its entrance blocked by a column that divides the door in two and creates an image of confusion which negatively impacts the flow of clients.

The best position for the owner or manager's desk is far from the main door and in the wealth area if possible. It should be placed in the power position with a view of the door, but not in line with it.

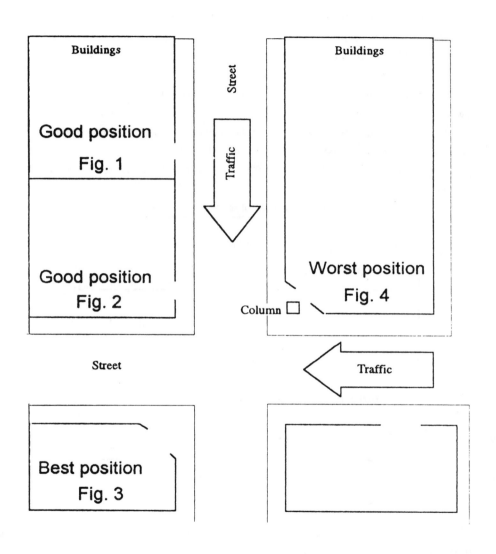

BUSINESS POSITIONS

A Business' Ba-Gua

The Ba-Gua is drawn or visualized over the layout of the business space with the «knowledge-profession-clients» areas always aligned with the main entrance. From here we can determine the location of each activity of the business, the owners and the employees. Each office also has its own Ba-Gua used in the same way as the Ba-Gua for the entire business. The entrance is always aligned with the line of water. For example, if an office located in the clients area (benefactors) of the general Ba-Gua is conflictive due to problems with its shape, differing personalities or other factors, this could effect the flow of energy and weaken client's behavior as well as the business' sales and income.

◀----------------- The back of the site -----------------▶

FINANCES	FAME	PARTNERS
FAMILY	HEALTH	CREATIVITY
KNOWLEDGE	PROFESSION	CLIENTS

◀-------- ALIGN WITH THE MAIN ENTRANCE ---------

A Business' Ba-Gau

Each office should align its individual Ba-Gua with its entrance door. If the office door is on a 90° angle with respect to the main door of the business, the office's Ba-Gua would be drawn on a 90° angle with respect to the Ba-Gua of the business.

Within the office, each desk has its own Ba-Gua with the line of water (knowledge, profession and benefactors) along the edge where the person sits.

50

All the Ba-Guas should work together to create an overall harmonious and balanced space. No Ba-Gua is more important than another. Small areas of disharmony, in a corner of a room or in a closet, can affect the people who live or work in the space.

The Colors of Feng Shui

In Feng Shui, each life area or activity has a corresponding color to reinforce it. For example, the knowledge area can be adjusted with objects, lights, surfaces or pictures in the color blue which will help improve cultural activities as well as self-development. If this decoration is reinforced with the Three Secrets, the results will be event better.

According to Master Lin Yun, the following colors are associated with each of the life areas:

LIFE AREAS	COLOR
Fame and reputation	Red
Marriage and relationships	Pink
Children and creativity	White
Benefactors	Gray
Career and profession	Black
Knowledge	Blue
Family relationships	Green
Finances	Purple

What clothes should I wear today? The color clothes you choose is based on your Chi and where you will be going. The color you pick will affect your mood throughout the day. In general, we choose a color according to our state of awareness on three levels: objective, subjective and transcendental.

Visualizing the Ba-Gua

The Ba-Gua is also a frame of reference associated with the theory of cycles and the colors of the elements with all their correspondences. When visualizing the Ba-Gua overlaid on a community, plot of land, house or work place, we can identify specific areas that correspond to each trigram. Every trigram symbolizes a color, an activity and a manifestation of the universal creative force or Chi. If we honor each area with the color, shape or energy that corresponds to it, we are reinforcing and encouraging the flow of creative energy.

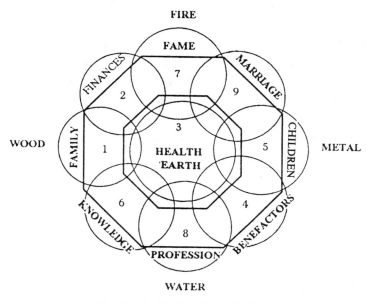

Lines and Circles of the Ba-Gua

The layout of the Ba-Gua's trigrams have a certain relationship with the «houses» used in astrological studies. In traditional astrology, twelve houses are used as a map of human activity. The twelve houses are distributed around the circle of the zodiac in relation to the cardinal points. The ascendant is positioned at the left-hand side of the natal chart, indicating where the sun rises each morning. It represents the cardinal direction east and corresponds to spring. The mid-heaven is the zenith of the sun in the sky in the south, radiating its intense heat and light. This position corresponds to summer and is represented in the upper part of the natal chart in house number ten. The descendent is the sun setting in the west; it corresponds to fall and is represented by the seventh house. The nadir is related to the north, night, winter and is associated with the fourth house which occupies the lowest point on the natal chart.

Traditional astrology uses as the solar year and the ecliptic as a frame of reference. The four cardinal houses are related to the Ba-Gua as follows:

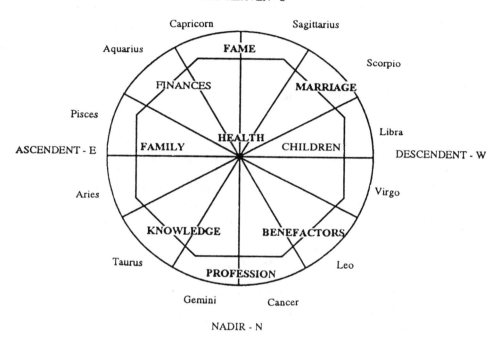

Ba-Gua and Astrological Correspondences

Each natal house covers an angle of approximately 30°.

Each trigram covers a 45° angle.

The Ba-Gua also symbolizes the control of the elements. Its four cardinal sides represent the four cardinal directions: east, south, west and north as follows:

1. Wood, east, family, the left. This side is identified as the «line of wood.»

2. Fire, south, fame, the upper part. This side is identified as the «line of fire.»
3. Metal, west, children, the right. This side is identified as the «line of metal.»
4. Water, north, profession, the lower part. This side is identified as the «line of water.»

ASTROLOGICAL HOUSES	FENG SHUI TRIGRAMS
1st house - East - Spring Ascendant - Left	Chen - East - Spring Wood - Left
10th house - South - Summer Mid-heaven - Above	Li - South - Summer Fire - Above
7th house - West - Fall Descendent - Right	Tui - West - Fall Metal - Right
4th house - North - Winter Nadir - Below	Khan - North - Winter Water - Below

Movements of the Ba-Gua

In Form School, visualizing or overlaying of the Ba-Gua does not take into account how the site or building is lined up with respect to the cardinal points: east, south, west and north. Instead, the Ba-Gua is always aligned according to the position of the «Mouth of Chi.»

The Mouth of Chi is where energy or vital life-force enters a building or space -the front door. Although other doors may be used more often in daily living, the front door is still used as the point of reference for aligning the Ba-Gua.

The Ba-Gua is always aligned with the line of water that is the extension of the Mouth of Chi. The octagonal figure is calculated by dividing the outside (perimeter) wall into three equal parts. If the space is rectangular, the Ba-Gua is adjusted to fit the symmetry of the space, though always maintaining its octagonal shape.

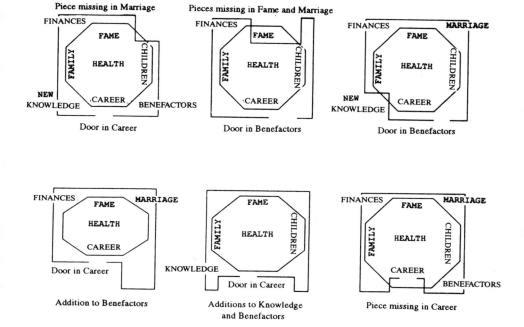

Placing the Lines of Harmony

It is very important to remember that Chi can only enter a space through the line of water, that is through the knowledge, profession or benefactors area.

The walls, ceilings and floors of a home are like a second skin that shields us from stormy weather and provides us with protection and privacy.

Structures, roofs, beams and walls determine how the Ba-Gua is overlaid.

The Ba-Gua should be visualized over the different areas of a property:

1. The Ba-Gua of the plot of land where the house is built.
2. The Ba-Gua of the lower floor of the structure.
3. The Ba-Gua of the various floors of the apartment or office building.
4. The Ba-Gua of each room.
5. The Ba-Gua of the bed and desk.

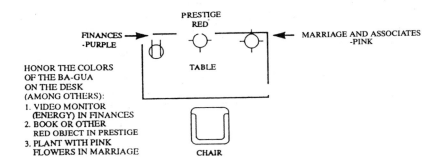

FINANCES → -PURPLE

PRESTIGE RED

MARRIAGE AND ASSOCIATES -PINK

HONOR THE COLORS
OF THE BA-GUA
ON THE DESK
(AMONG OTHERS):
1. VIDEO MONITOR
   (ENERGY) IN FINANCES
2. BOOK OR OTHER
   RED OBJECT IN PRESTIGE
3. PLANT WITH PINK
   FLOWERS IN MARRIAGE

TABLE

CHAIR

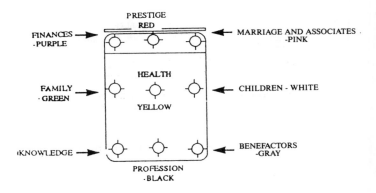

PRESTIGE RED

FINANCES → -PURPLE

MARRIAGE AND ASSOCIATES -PINK

HEALTH

FAMILY → · GREEN

YELLOW

CHILDREN - WHITE

KNOWLEDGE →

PROFESSION -BLACK

BENEFACTORS -GRAY

The Ba-Gua of a Bed

6. Others (The Ba-Gua of furniture, dressers, cabinets, gardens, bodies, cars, hands, etc...)

The Ba-Gua is always visualized in the same way, fame is at the top and profession is at the bottom aligned with the main door or Mouth of Chi.

The method for visualizing the Ba-Gua of a house, plot of land or building is as follows:

1. Find the position of the Mouth of Chi, that is, the main door of the building, even if it is rarely used.

2. Extend the line of the main entrance.

3. Draw or visualize the Ba-Gua over the house's floor plan aligning the line of water (knowledge to the left, profession in the middle and benefactors to the right) with the main door, the entrance for the creative force, the Mouth of Chi.

It is important to note that the main entrance, or Mouth of Chi, can only be located along the life areas of knowledge, profession or benefactors despite the shape of the space.

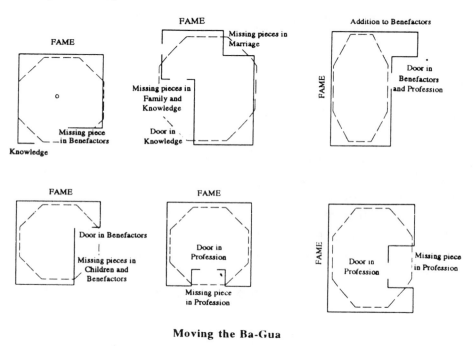

Moving the Ba-Gua

Factors Influencing the Ba-Gua

When overlaying the Ba-Gua on a space. a number of things may happen:

1. Missing areas
2. Areas that have been expanded or added on to
3. Areas outside the Ba-Gua

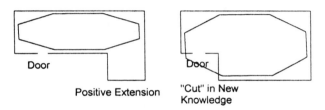

Door

Positive Extension

Door

"Cut" in New
Knowledge

«L» SHAPED HOUSES: WHEN THE WALL WHERE THE MAIN
ENTRANCE IS LOCATED IS LESS THAN HALF THE LENGTH OF
THAT SIDE OF THE HOUSE, THE LINE OF WATER OF THE BA-GUA
EXTENDS ALONG THE LONGEST WALL OF THAT SIDE WHICH
RESULTS IN MISSING PIECES.

«L-shaped» houses

1. Missing areas

«L» shaped, zigzag or other irregularly shaped spaces create missing
pieces. The area that extends out will be an addition to the space or a missing
piece depending on its length. If the length of the extended piece is half or more
of the total length of that side of the house, the octagon is extended to the
outside wall of that area. In doing so an empty space or missing piece is created.
If the length of the extended area is less than half of the total length of that
side of the house, the octagon is aligned with the length of longer wall, creating
an extension.

As solutions for missing pieces, the following adjustments may be used:

1. Bright objects.
   a) Lights - When you have access to the area that is missing on the
      exterior, install a flood light in the corner of the missing area and
      point it at the roof.
   b) Mirrors - On the inside, hang mirrors on either side of the walls.
   c) Crystal balls - Hang a crystal ball on the edge of the corner inside
      the home.
2. Heavy objects. Place a statue on the corner of the missing area
   outside.
3. Life energy. Plants or trees with vibrant colors that correspond to
   that area can be planted.
4. Others.

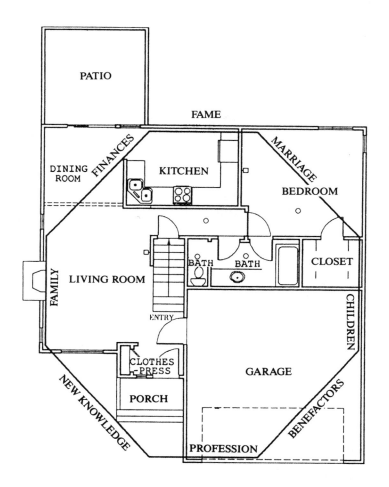

Overlaying the Ba-Gua on a living space. In this example, the line of water has been moved to the longest wall on the side of the house with the main entrance.

2. Additions or extended areas

Areas that are extended or have additions are beneficial and tend to increase or strengthen the activity related to the area where they are found.

3. Areas outside the Ba-Gua

When an area that falls outside the Ba-Gua is separated architecturally from the house's structure -or when a wall that separates the area from the rest of the house falls outside the Ba-Gua- instead of being an extension, it is considered as outside the Ba-Gua. Solution: Hang a mirror on the adjacent wall, or hang a mirror on the wall parallel to the area that you want to reintegrate into the main Ba-Gua.

Remember that the Ba-Gua is always aligned with the fame area in the upper portion of the space, the profession area in the center of the lower wall, family to the left, and children to the right.

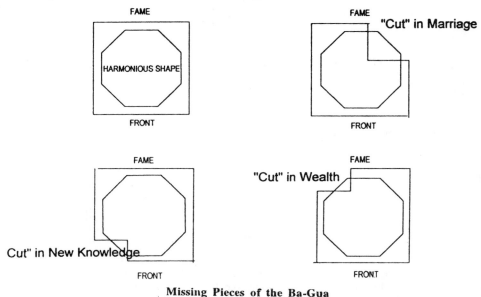

Missing Pieces of the Ba-Gua

Areas and Objects within the Ba-Gua

An atrium or central patio located in the Tai Chi, or center of the Ba-Gua, is beneficial.

Having the bathroom in the areas that correspond to the fire element (finances, fame and marriage) and in the center of the space is conflictive. Solutions: 1) Hang a mirror on the outside of the bathroom door. 2) Place live plants inside the bathroom. 3) If there are windows, hang curtains in the color that corresponds to area where the bathroom is located. 4) Others.

Kitchens are conflictive in areas that correspond to the water elemen (knowledge, profession and benefactors) and in the center. Solutions: 1) Hang mirrors behind the burners on the stove top. 2) Place plants here to balance the elements and hang mirrors on the outside walls of the kitchen, if possible, to eliminate the negative effects on this area.

A fireplace is wonderful for its light and central heat. Place plants on either side if there is furniture positioned around it.

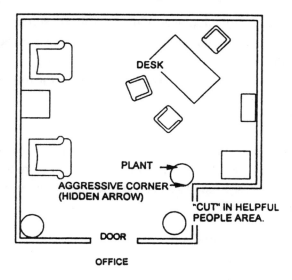

OFFICE

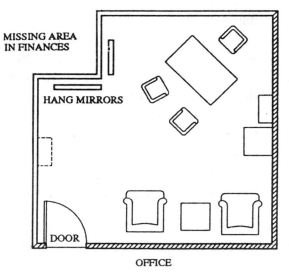

OFFICE

A water fountain is good. Its position of strength is in the water area (knowledge, profession and benefactors). It reinforces Chi when it is in the center of the house.

Beds and desks should never be in line with the door. Solutions:

1) Move the bed to the power position (opposite and on a diagonal from the door, out of the entrance path of Chi while still maintaining a view of the door).
2) If the bed cannot be moved, place a Chinese folding screen at the foot of the bed, and hang a mirror so that someone who is in the bed has a view of door.
3) Hang a wind chime or Feng Shui crystal ball between the foot of the bed and the door.
4) Others.

Any situation or condition that drains energy produces a loss of opportunity in luck, finances and health. Energy loss can result from toilets, fireplaces, chimney flues, doors, windows and other openings. Chi can be lost in the following situations:

- Front and back door are aligned.
- Bathroom in the center of the house.
- Bathroom next to the front door.
- Bathroom over the entrance.
- Bathrooms on the line of fire (finances, fame and marriage)
- Nearby streets that curve away from the house.
- Nearby river that curves away from the house.
- Homes located on a bay.
- Broken windows, screens, doors, roofs and other structures.
- Dry plants and tree stumps in front of the house drain energy from benefactors, profession and knowledge. Dry plants inside drain happiness as well as physical and mental stability.
- Water or gas leaks and leaks in the roof.

Another common situation is a blocking or biting wall. Blocks create stagnant energy and can generate confusion, lack of concentration and loss of work or opportunities. Among the most common blockages are the following:

- Trees, columns or walls that block the outside of the front door.
- A front door that is sealed or blocked for lack of use.
- Columns, walls or furniture that block the view of the main door.
- Entrance doors hidden behind walls or structures, or located in closed off areas.
- Doors that are below street level.
- Noisy windows that do not open properly.
- Front doors that are blocked, that don't open freely.
- Doors that open onto closed off areas.
- Trees in front of windows or patio doors.

Another situation that is commonly found in houses is aggressive shapes such as corners of columns and walls, irregular structures and exposed beams. Among aggressive structural design features are:

- Slanted or angled walls and ceilings. (Adjust these with Chinese bamboo flutes, horizontal decoration, curtains, among others.)
- Spiral staircases in the center of the home.
- Staircases that are in line with or biting the entrance door.
- The corners of columns and walls pointing at the entrance.
- Beams that cut the kitchen or bedroom.
- Patio doors (back doors) aligned with the front door.

A curved pool that hugs the house is protective. However, if it is angular and points toward the house, its aggressive affect should be adjusted by placing rounded planters or plants between the pool and the house.

Frequently there are conflicts in the distribution of the elements within the design of the house. Among the most common are:

- Fire (the kitchen, pyramid, red, square, fireplace) in the center (earth) of the house.

- Fire (the kitchen, pyramid, red, square, fireplace) in the front (water) of the house.
- Fire (the kitchen, pyramid, red, square, fireplace) on the right side (metal) of the house.
- Water (pool, bathroom, black furniture) in the back (fire) of the house.
- Water (pool, bathroom, black furniture) in the center (earth) of the house.

Decorating with Feng Shui

Feng Shui is practiced by each person according to his or her knowledge and experience. Everyone has their own system and method for working. This book illustrates a process that can be used both on a personal and a professional level.

Physical Category (Sying)

The following are some visible observations that we should consider when doing a Feng Shui study.

1. The Chi of the land
* The shape of the land, rivers, lakes, oceans, hills, mountains.
* The presence of animals, a variety of birds.
* The type of vegetation, the vitality of the land, the presence of lush vegetation.
* Paths, geological zones, wells, mineral deposits and underground waterways.

2. The location of the space
* A house that is on top of a mountain is exposed to unexpected climatic changes and is in a risky location.
* A house that is at the very front of a plot of land is in a weak position.
* A house located in the center of the plot is in a beneficial position.
* A house located near a cemetery or airport is in a risky position.

BUILDING "C" IS VERY EXPOSED

C

GOOD CHI

PHYSICAL AND SPIRITUAL
ABUNDANCE

A   B

TRIANGULAR HILL

**Buildings on a hill. Buy the plots on the sides,
preferably in areas «A» or «B.»**

3. Technological influences

* Streets, bridges, highways, railroads.
* Electrical lines, transformers.
* Airports, cemeteries, industrial zones.

4. The shape of the plot of land

* Rectangular, square and round plots are positive.
* Irregular shaped plots need to be studied.
* A plot in the shape of an animal is considered positive.
* A parcel that is very open is considered vulnerable.

5. The shape of the house

* Houses shaped like objects or animals are generally considered positive.
* Square and rectangular shaped homes are positive.
* «L» shapes and boot shapes have weakened effects in certain areas based on the lines of harmony of the Ba-Gua.
* In homes with missing pieces, additions or expansions can be positive if the adjacent wall is inside the structure of the house. If not, it has a weakening effect.

6. The main door
* This is the mouth where Chi enters.
* Observe the line of water and the three possible entrances.
* The entrance path to the front door.
* Objects that obstruct the Mouth of Chi such as trees or columns.
* Light and sound around the Mouth of Chi.

7. The layout of the rooms
* The initial view from the main entrance looking in and looking out.
* The central line of the house. Areas of Yang and Yin. The reception, study and entertainment areas should be in front of the center line. The kitchen and family areas, quiet areas and bedrooms should be behind the center line.
* The location of the lines of harmony of the Ba-Gua.
* Moving the lines of harmony of the Ba-Gua horizontally and vertically.
* The location of the bathrooms on the ground floor and the upper floors.
* The location of the kitchen.
* The location of the fireplace.
* The hallways.
* Lights and colors.

8. Structural designs
* Aggressive walls and corners.
* Walls that close off hallways.
* Slanted walls.
* Exposed beams.
* Square columns with aggressive corners.
* Slanted ceiling.

9. Staircases
* Staircases aligned with the main entrance.
* Spiral staircases.
* Open staircases.
* Narrow staircases.
* Landings on staircases.

10. Doors and windows

* Doors that don't «talk to each other.» (doors that are facing but not directly aligned)
* Conflicting doors.
* Sealed doors.
* Biting doors.
* Windows.

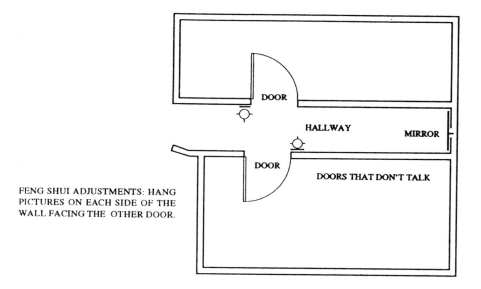

FENG SHUI ADJUSTMENTS: HANG PICTURES ON EACH SIDE OF THE WALL FACING THE OTHER DOOR.

11. Surfaces

* The finishes on surfaces, the material and products used, natural or synthetic.
* Tiles, wall paper and paint.

12. The Fixtures

* The plumbing, the bathrooms, the sinks.
* The electrical wiring, the lights.
* The door handles, noisy or broken hinges.
* Broken windows or screens.
* The upkeep of the plants and garden.
* The water filtration system, how the roof is maintained.
* General upkeep.

13. Furniture and decorative objects
* The position of the bed.
* The position of the desks.
* The location of the pictures, art objects and books.
* The location of electronic equipment.

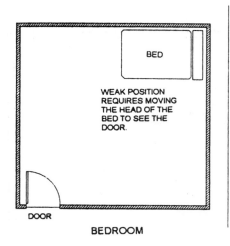

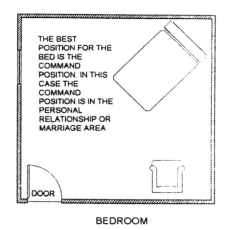

BEDROOM   BEDROOM

14. Others
* Construction materials.
* Bau-Biologie.
* Others.

Although each student develops his own system, it is necessary to always follow a certain work method. After analyzing the space and identifying areas that need attention, the next step is to use the decorative suggestions, the principles of the tradition, the Nine Minor Additions and, when necessary, transcendental methods.

According the Tibetan Tantric Buddhism, the method chosen should consider the visible or tangible factors as well as the invisible or intangible factors. After having observed and analyzed the space, the practitioner should determine the necessary adjustments needed to harmonize the space. These adjustments can be chosen from among the Nine Minor Adjustments, and other traditional principles. When the changes are reinforced with transcendental solutions, the Feng Shui decoration will produce a result of 120%. The method can be summarized as follows:

Visible Factors (tangible)

1. The Chi of the space
2. The shape of the land
3. The shape of the house or building
4. The layout of the home

The visible factors can be divided in external (Yang) factors and internal (Yin) factors.

Among external factors are:
1. Bridges
2. Electrical lines
3. Buildings
4. Noise
5. Transformers
6. Subterranean installations
7. Underground factors

Among internal factors are:
1. Position of beds
2. Position of kitchen
3. Exposed beams
4. Staircases
5. Columns
6. Desks
7. Colors

Invisible Factors (intangibles)

1. History of the space.
2. Environmental quality space.
3. Geomagnetic energy.
4. Environmental quality of the area.
5. Others.

After observing and analyzing the place, the practitioner determines the adjustments that are necessary to balance and create a harmonious environment. The solutions can be external (Sying) or internal or transcendental (Yi.)

Analysis of External Factors

The principle objective of Feng Shui is to activate Chi so that it does not stagnate.

Positive Chi flows in harmonious curves like the magnetic lines of the poles and the gravitational force fields that emanate from the Earth, Sun, Moon and the planets. Negative Chi, known as Sha, moves in straight lines and can manifest suddenly or slowly.

Usually anything that manifests in a convex shape is masculine (Yang) and anything that manifests in a concave form is feminine (Yin).

Whatever shape, symbolic or real, that corresponds to the elements fire and air (elements that cannot be contained) are masculine (Yang). Any shape that corresponds to the elements water and earth (elements that can be contained) are feminine (Yin).

The ideal proportion of Yang elements to Yin is three to one. For example, a valley (Yin), protected on three sides by mountains (Yang) with the southern exposure open (Yin) is a classic example of positive Chi.

Chi continually fluctuates in urban areas and can change its polarity in very short distances.

The shape of land plots and houses is very important. There should be similar proportions between the shape of the land and the shape of the house constructed on it.

Circles, rectangles and squares are good shapes.

Remember that the flow of Chi isn't just the flow of energy, but that of friends, information, money and many other forms of riches.

The following are some recommendations for analyzing a space. With practice, the student will begin awakening his/her intuitive and observational Feng Shui skills.

The Neighborhood

It is a good idea to look over the structures, buildings and how property is used in the area surrounding the home or business that you are studying or planning to buy. A house that is close to a slaughter house or cemetery will be influenced by adverse emanations. A tall building that is close to a home causes blocked energy and could affect the evolution, health and careers of those living in the home. When the offending building is very large, it is a good idea to hang a convex mirror, with the trigrams on it, to eliminate the effect of the negative energy that is being focused on the home.

Observe the shape of the structures that are around the area. Use the elemental correspondences as a guide. Conical shapes correspond to the fire element. Arch shapes correspond to metal. Shapes that are vertically cylindrical, like most tall buildings, are the wood element. Structures with flat roofs are earth element.

If the terrain is very flat, Chi tends to stagnate.

In general, a house that is near a confluence of rivers or lakes, or close to the ocean will receive excellent Chi.

Selecting the Site

Humanity's evolution is intimately tied to Earth itself. The history of man has been lost through time. Cultures of the past flourished on river banks, mountains and ocean shores. We do not have records of ancient civilizations beyond what we know of the Egyptians, Amorites, Hittites and Chinese cultures that existed some 4,000 years before our own. The development of ancient civilizations depended on the organization of their social structure, of choosing fertile lands and the presence of rivers and lakes. The success or failure of cultures, cities, towns and hamlets was closely linked to the presence of energy sources, forests, minerals and animals as well as the shape and elevation of the terrain, lakes and seas. The beauty of the mountains harmonized with the valleys, rivers, lakes and the sea.

Frequently, when we visit a city or country that we have never been to, there seems to something that evokes memories or certain feelings in us. That unique something leads us to consider the existence of an energetic presence that receives us, a presence that is a combination of all the vibrations that make up that place. The visible shapes and colors show us what the place is like, while our intuition picks up on feelings and subtle impressions of an energy that speaks to us of the culture and people that live or have lived in that land. This essence, that transcends the buildings and monuments, reflects the emanations of a subtle yet powerful energy -the universal life-force of creation, Chi.

The art of using Feng Shui within spaces grows from learning to perceive this energy. Chi, moving in spirals, following curves, avoiding angles, is projected from the Universe and radiates from Earth. Chi circulates through different vibratory layers of our planet harmoniously manifesting shapes and life in all its forms. When Chi circulates harmoniously on the surface, the Earth is imbued with fertility and a pleasant climate.

The purpose of modern Feng Shui, the Fourth Level as taught by Master Lin Yun, is the same as always: to find places that provide the best environment for people to live or work in.

Frequently, modern urbanization affects the Feng Shui of a space. Tall buildings with aggressive shapes and colors that do not coordinate, cut into the natural scenery and contribute to environmental deterioration.

When choosing a place to build a house, observe how Chi manifests in the environment:

If the vegetation is green and abundant, there is good Chi. If there are many trees and plants with dried or yellowing leaves, it means that Chi is escaping from the surface of Earth and that plant life is being affected.

Peaceful animals such as pets, birds and deer are signs of good Chi. Wild dogs and animals, crows and rats are indications of the absence of it.

Those who live in a particular area also affect its Chi. How a neighborhood looks is an indication of the type of energy that emanates from those who live there. When buying or renting a home or a business space, it is good to know its history. It tells us if those who lived there before where happy or unhappy, successful or not. If a business shut down due to bankruptcy, it is a sign of poor quality Chi. If the previous occupants moved to a better place, it is a sign that they received good Chi in that place.

The Natural Shapes of the Land

The ancient Chinese believed that all life was part of a larger, living organism that made up Earth and Universe, forming one vital body. They used animal symbolism to describe mountains, valleys, rivers and lakes. For them, a mountain could represent a dragon, elephant, phoenix or tiger. Over time, these ideas developed into a spatial art that served as the basis for the Form School of Feng Shui.

Mountains are generally studied with three of the most common shapes in mind: a) round b) square) triangular.

When the slope of a mountain is gentle, covered with good vegetation and ends in valley it signals a good place to build a house.

When houses are built in the side of the mountain, they receive protective energy from it. If the vegetation on the mountain slopes is abundant, rich in color and fertile it means that positive Chi is present. According to the traditions of Feng Shui, building a house on the top of a mountain is dangerous. It is exposed to the severity of weather, wind, and unforeseen events that occur to those who live there such as changes in jobs, dangerous accidents and operations.

Highways and Streets

Highways are like rivers as their vital energy flows and feeds our technological civilization. Streets are like capillaries that carry energy to each house or cell of the body of our civilization. Streets beautify a neighborhood when they are clean and designed with green boulevards and trees. The principles of the tradition show us which types of streets have negative effects on those who live on them.

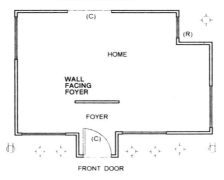

SLIDING GLASS DOORS

(C)

(R)

HOME

WALL
FACING
FOYER

FOYER

(C)

FRONT DOOR

STREET

"T" INTERSECTION IN FRONT
OF A HOME IS DETRIMENTAL.
SOLUTIONS: HANG A FLAG,
OR INSTALL A WATER
FOUNTAIN, OR WIND MILL,
OR BA-GUA, OR OTHER
SOLUTION IN FRONT OF THE
HOUSE. REINFORCE WITH
THE THREE SECRETS.

Bad Feng Shui

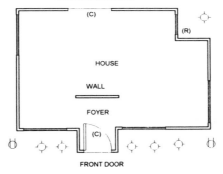

SLIDING GLASS DOORS.

(C)

(R)

HOUSE

WALL

FOYER

(C)

FRONT DOOR

STREET THAT ENDS IN
FRONT OF A PIECE OF PROPERTY

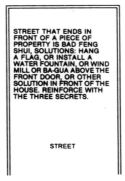

STREET THAT ENDS IN
FRONT OF A PIECE OF
PROPERTY IS BAD FENG
SHUI, SOLUTIONS: HANG
A FLAG, OR INSTALL A
WATER FOUNTAIN, OR WIND
MILL OR BA-GUA ABOVE THE
FRONT DOOR, OR OTHER
SOLUTION IN FRONT OF THE
HOUSE. REINFORCE WITH
THE THREE SECRETS.

STREET

Bad Feng Shui

1. A house built on the end of a street is subject to secret arrows, sudden changes and unforeseen accidents. The front of the house should be protected by installing a water fountain, hanging flags, a Ba-Gua mirror or other solutions.

2. Streets that curve away from the house create an energetic void that drains energy from the corresponding areas. If the street curves away from the right side of the house (wood), it could cause sickness, mental confusion and financial difficulties. If the street curves away from the left side of the house, energy could be drained from personal relationships, relations with children and friendships. These effects can be balanced by using mirrors, flags, Ba-Gua mirrors and other solutions to reinforce and raise the house's Chi.

3. Houses that are on dead-end streets, on T-intersections or "V" shaped intersections are subject to financial problems, difficulties in personal and family relations and sickness. They should be protected with adjustments similar to those mentioned above. The same is true for a house built below street level.

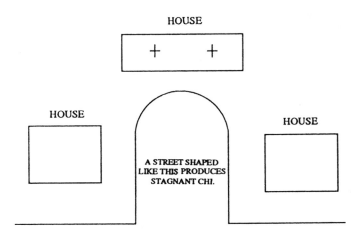

The Land

Choosing a house begins with the land. The location of the property, the shape of the land, the energy and the setting are among the principle factors in selecting or studying a place. The best land shapes are: square, rectangular or round. If the land is in the shape of an animal, it is considered good luck.

To overlay the Ba-Gua on the land, we must first determine the entrance of the property. This is known as the «Chi Kou» or Mouth of Chi. The entrance is aligned with the line of water of the Ba-Gua and should be in the area of knowledge, profession or benefactors.

It is good to honor the colors of the trigrams in each area of the land plot. In Sun, the area of finances, purple or violet colored plants should be grown. In Li, the fame area, plants with red flowers should be used. Plants with thorns, whose cone-shaped form symbolizes fire, should be planted in the back of the house. Pink flowers are good in Kun, the marriage area, and so on.

A house protected by hills or mountains to the sides and back and with a valley in front has an ideal location. This position is known as the "pearl in the oyster" or "the two dragons and the pearl."

The shape of the land should not interfere with the natural landscape.

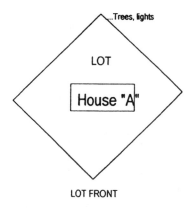

The building should be facing the sraight sides of irregular shaped lots. If the house is already built, install lights, flags or wind milds in the corner areas, aligned with front and back doors. Reinforce with the Three Secrets.

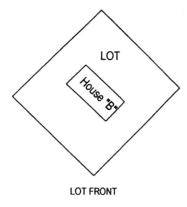

A house in a diamong-shaped lot should be built toward the middle of the lot with the front of the house parallel to one of the sides of the lot.

Diamond Shaped Plots

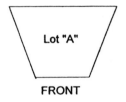

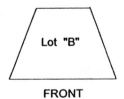

Propitious shape. Construction toward the middle of the lot.

Unpropitious shaped lot, the back is narrower than the front, producing stagnation and blockage of the vital life force, Ch'i. Recommendations: Placing lights, or trees in each of the corners in the back of the lot. Reinforce with the Three Secrets.

Irregularly Shaped Plots

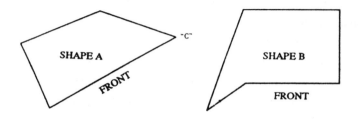

SHAPE "A" IS AGGRESSIVE TOWARD SHAPE "B." POINT "C" FORMS A SECRET ARROW POINTED AT PROPERTY "B." PROTECT PROPERTY "B" WITH A BA-GUA THAT FACES THE CORNER, OR PLACE A HEAVY OBJECT OR FENCE THAT SOFTENS THE AGGRESSIVE EFFECT OF THE CORNER. REINFORCE WITH THE THREE SECRETS.

Plot or Building Shapes

The shape of the land is less important than the size and shape of the house built on it.

When land has an irregular shape with one side that is much narrower than the rest, you can plant bamboo or leafy trees there, or install a light to balance the irregularity.

Rectangles, squares or circles are generally good.

Use lights to remedy irregular shapes or to fill spaces left empty due to different elevations.

Plant bushes and trees in the north and west to neutralize negative Chi and thoughts.

The Shape of the House

According to Feng Shui design, shapes mold our lives. Our lives are contained within our houses; our lives as Yang, our houses as Yin.

The shape of the house is intimately related to the people that live there. The doors represent the mouth, the windows the eyes, the hallways the arteries and veins through which vital life force or Chi flows.

A house that is rectangular, square or round is prosperous. U and L shaped houses always have areas that are missing, which produces a weakening of the energy flowing to the affected areas. This type of design is common in the U.S. especially in the southern states.

A house should have a spacious front door (double doors) and be free of obstructions like big trees, small buildings, or straight and narrow entrance paths aligned with the front door.

When a pool, which represents the water element, is located behind the house, along the line of fire, it can affect the fame and reputation of those who live there. A solution would be to install a green fence or place green plants between the pool and the house. Reinforce with the Three Secrets.

A pool that curves and hugs the house is protective. If the pool is on an angle, the pointing corner puts pressure on the house and produces a conflict of shapes. To solve this problem, place heavy objects or planters to balance and soften the aggressive shape of the pool.

A house or an apartment built below street level can negatively affect health and careers. To remedy this situation, you can install a spot light that illuminates the highest point on the roof of the house. Or, lights can be placed in the four corners of the roof.

The Front Door

According to Black Hat School, the three main areas of the house are:

1. The main door
2. The master bedroom
3. The kitchen

The entrance is the first area that should be studied. What is seen from the front door is very important, more important than which way the door opens. The first room seen from the front door affects the habits of the people who live there and determines how they will respond to life events.

For example, if the first thing that you see from the front door is the kitchen, it is possible that those who live there will tend to overeat.

When the kitchen is next to the front door, it can cause digestive problems for those living there. A Feng Shui solution is to place a bookshelf in view of the door. The symbolism of the books will influence the subconscious minds of those entering to read or study instead of eat.

If the first thing seen upon entering is the television, the tendency will be to connect with it. Objects, sounds, shapes, colors, fragrances and energy speak to our subconscious each time we open the door to our secondary body, our home.

If the first thing we see when we come in is a wall, a message of obstruction will immediately be sent to our subconscious, producing emotional responses such as headaches, fatigue, general malaise, and a sense that our lives are blocked. There are a number of ways to solve this situation. Hang a mirror on the wall to open this area up. The mirror should be hung so that the top is above the head of the tallest member of the family; the head should never be cut off from view. Other solutions would be to decorate the wall with a flower arrangement or a picture of a landscape.

Among some common problems found in the entrance area are:

1. Entrance blocked by a column. If the column is inside the house and square, it can be mirrored to eliminate the negative effect, or a plant or decorative statue can be placed in front of it to soften its aggressive corners. Another solution is to hang a small crystal ball 9 inches or 9 cm from the ceiling in line with the aggressive corner. If the column is outside, a plant can be placed in front of it or it can be decorated with climbing vines, or a transcendental solution can be used.

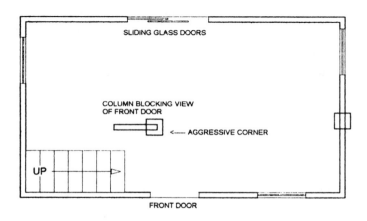

SLIDING GLASS DOORS

COLUMN BLOCKING VIEW
OF FRONT DOOR

<—— AGGRESSIVE CORNER

UP

FRONT DOOR

2. A very common situation is a split view. This occurs when we come in the door and are met by a wall that partially blocks our view. If the wall creating the split view is on the left side as we look in, our left eye will be focused on the wall that is right in front of us, while the right eye will be focusing in the distance (or vice versa). This variation in focus produces confusion and disharmony. To resolve it, decorate the wall with flowers or a picture of a landscape or wide-open spaces; or hang a mirror on the wall and a wind chime between the door and the wall creating the split view.

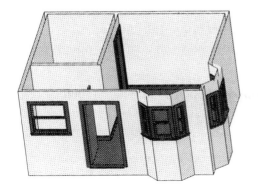

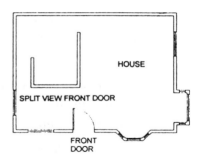

HOUSE

SPLIT VIEW FRONT DOOR

FRONT
DOOR

The front door should open onto a spacious area.

When the front door is in line with a sliding glass door to the back, Chi can be lost. This lost energy will have repercussions on friendships, children may leave home quickly, and money enters and leaves rapidly. Some possible solutions are: 1) Decorate with plants, especially those with trunks. Place them around the area with the sliding glass doors. 2) Hang crystal balls at the entrance door (9 units from the ceiling) and in the center of the sliding glass doors. 3) Place flower arrangements or decorative sculptures to enhance the area. Reinforce with the Three Secrets.

A kitchen or bathroom near the entrance weakens vital energy and affects the health of those who live there.

PROBLEMS:
KITCHEN AND BATHROOM
NEXT TO THE ENTRANCE

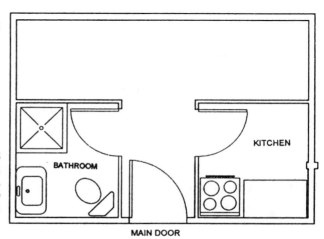

SOLUTIONS:
HANG MIRRORS ON THE DOORS
OF THE BATH AND KITCHEN;
HANG A FENG SHUI CRYSTAL
BALL IN THE BATHROOM AND
KITCHEN. DECORATE WITH
PLANTS AND FLOWERS.

BATHROOM

KITCHEN

MAIN DOOR

81

Important points concerning the front door of the home:

Chi always enters through the front door, even if another door is used 99% of the time.

It doesn't matter which way the door opens, but what is seen
  a) looking in.
  b) looking out.

What is the Mouth of Chi in an office building or apartment complex? The entrance to the building.

Doors

A door that opens toward a wall restricts the flow of Chi, weakening the amount of energy in the area of the Ba-Gua where the door is. To solve this, hang a mirror on the wall to increase the space, making it appear bigger, or install a light or hang a wind chime that makes sound when the door is opened.

Door alignment within a home is very important in Feng Shui. Avoid having two bathroom doors facing one another.

Doors that are not aligned can be cured by hanging mirrors or pictures on the wall facing the door.

A door at the end of a long hallway puts the health of those who live in the house at risk. Hang a mirror on the door or the wall at the end of the hallway to activate the flow of Chi bringing prosperity and progress for the family.

The proportion of doors to windows in a house is also important in Feng Shui design as it affects the relationship between parents and children. The recommended ratio of windows to doors is no more than a 3:1. Doors represent respect for parents, and windows are the children's voices. To improve family relationships and to maintain harmony in the home, hang a small bell on the front door, or a wind chime in front of it so it makes sound when the door is opened.

A door located in the back of the house in the fame area can drain the family's reputation. Reinforce it with Chinese bamboo flutes, crystal balls or other decorative Feng Shui objects. Reinforce it with the Three Secrets.

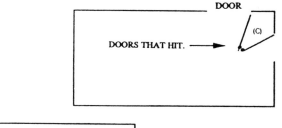

DOOR

DOORS THAT HIT. ———▶

(C)

SOLUTION:
HANG A FENG SHUI CRYSTAL
BALL AT POINT «C» OR ATTACH
2 CM RED CIRCLES ON THE
IMPACT POINT, OR OTHER
SOLUTIONS. REINFORCE WITH
THE THREE SECRETS.

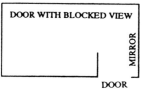

DOOR WITH BLOCKED VIEW

MIRROR

DOOR

THE ENTRANCE SHOULD LOOK
INTO OPEN SPACES.
SOLUTIONS: HANG A MIRROR
OR A PICTURE WITH A LAND-
SCAPE.

DOOR ON A SLANT

DOOR

A DOOR ON A SLANT IS CON-
FLICTIVE. SOLUTION: HANG
TWO WIND CHIMES OR CRYS-
TAL BALLS. ONE INSIDE AND
ONE OUTSIDE THE DOOR

Doors

Windows

The top of the window frame should be higher that the tallest person living in the house; if not, it could cause depression in the person whose energy is being cut off.

When a bed is aligned with a window, especially in apartments on upper floors, a small Feng Shui crystal ball should be hung in it.

Windows should be kept in good condition. Broken glass and window jambs weaken the corresponding area of the Ba-Gua and create a loss or drain of energy.

The Master Bedroom

The second important area is the master bedroom. It represents the energy that nurtures the spiritual stability of the home. Often, more attention is paid to other areas such as the living room or dining room, but the bedroom should be as neatly kept and cared for as the rest of the house. Missing pieces in the lines of harmony, columns, aggressive corners, and the alignment of doors in the master bedroom affect the harmony of those who represent the center and heart of the family and could have repercussions on their physical and spiritual health.

The position of the bed is very important. It is conflictive to sleep with the feet pointing toward the door of the bedroom. The bed should be in the command position, so those who sleep there have a view of the door.

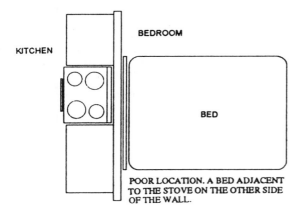

KITCHEN

BEDROOM

BED

POOR LOCATION. A BED ADJACENT TO THE STOVE ON THE OTHER SIDE OF THE WALL.

SOLUTIONS:
1- HANG A MIRROR BEHIND THE BURNERS.
2 - MOVE THE HEAD OF THE BED IF POSSIBLE.
3 - HANG A 9 CM OCTAGONAL MIRROR BEHIND THE BED, FACING THE KITCHEN.
REINFORCE WITH THE THREE SECRETS.

The Kitchen

The third important area in the house, according to Feng Shui, is the kitchen. It represents prosperity. This is where meals that give energy to those who live there are prepared. Feng Shui gives special importance to the kitchen in creating harmony, happiness and prosperity in the house.

The tradition suggests hanging a mirror behind the burners to double the number, usually from four to eight. As the burners are the source of preparing food, they should all be used, in rotation, to insure that the Chi of prosperity does not stagnate. The quality of food contributes to the flow of Chi in our bodies.

84

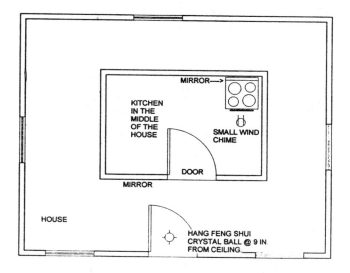

A small wind chime should be hung on the ceiling above the stove where the person who cooks the meals stands. The wind chime elevates the Chi of the person cooking which in turn is transferred to those who eat the food. The Chi of the cook can affect the health of the family members.

Even if the burners are not used for cooking very often, it is a good idea to turn on at least one of them a day, if only to heat water. Alternate among the burners.

The best area for the kitchen is in the fame area, unless the stove can be seen from the front door. A good location for the kitchen is anywhere along the line of fire or wood. A kitchen in the center of the house can affect the mental and physical health of those who live there. This situation can be remedied by hanging mirrors. There are also other transcendental solutions to alleviate this situation. The best solution will be the one that comes to mind as the practitioner is doing the Feng Shui.

Keep the burners clean. Dirty burners cause financial difficulty.

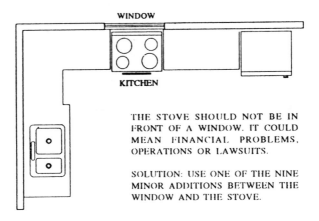

WINDOW

KITCHEN

THE STOVE SHOULD NOT BE IN FRONT OF A WINDOW. IT COULD MEAN FINANCIAL PROBLEMS, OPERATIONS OR LAWSUITS.

SOLUTION: USE ONE OF THE NINE MINOR ADDITIONS BETWEEN THE WINDOW AND THE STOVE.

Stove tops located in front of a window can cause financial difficulties, sickness, operations and lawsuits.

Burners aligned with or behind the central line of the house (parallel to the front and back) are in a fortunate position.

In «boot» shaped kitchens, the stove top should be in the «sole.»

Burners that are broken, dirty or unused weaken Chi and bring bad luck.

The person cooking should not have their back to the door when they stand at the stove.

Kitchens located on the line of fire (finances, fame and marriage) are fortunate, except if they are facing doors or are bitten by them. It is good fortune for the kitchen to be located in an addition to the line of fire in the finances area (as long as it is not opposite a door or being bitten by one). However, it is conflictive if the kitchen is located in an addition to fame or marriage.

It is conflictive if the stove top is located on the other side of the wall from a toilet or a bed.

A full pantry reflects good Chi.

Structural Design, Walls and Columns

Edges and corners are considered harmful and unfortunate. Hang a mirror on one or both sides of the corner. Hang a vine on the edge or a Feng Shui crystal ball in front of it.

Columns play an important role in Feng Shui interior decoration. Round columns are acceptable and should be decorated with colors and materials that are harmonious with the space. Square columns are dangerous.

Solutions: Mirror the sides of the column or hang vines along the edges to soften them. Reinforce with the Three Secrets.

Stairways

Staircases going up or down, that face the entrance door, have an unbalancing and blocking effect. According to the tradition, any staircase aligned with or that is biting the main door is a source of conflict. The energy of the house, commercial center or office, will be affected when the staircase faces the front entrance. The Chinese avoid this situation as it causes Chi and money to roll away from the space. To balance this situation, there are a number of decorative adjustments you can make: 1) Hang a Feng Shui crystal ball between the door and the staircase. 2) Hang a wind chime in front of the staircase and in line with the front door. 3) Decorate the staircase with vines that give the impression of moving upwards. 4) Hang a round crystal light fixture above the staircase.

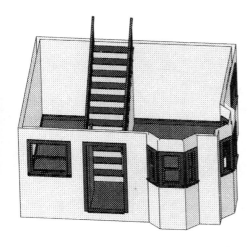

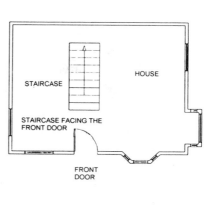

All spiral staircases are conflictive. Their shape acts as a corkscrew. The blocked energy often affects the health of family members, showing up as headaches, heart attacks, insomnia, anxiety and miscarriages. To resolve the effects of this type of staircase, there are a number of decorative solutions: 1) Place plants on the side and at the base of the stairs and hang a mirror facing the last stair on the upper floor (if there is a wall there). 2) A crystal ball can be hung at the top, just after the last stair. 3) Hang a crystal ball or a wind chime in front of the staircase. The stairs should be wide and well lit so that energy flows freely between the two floors.

Staircase landings are also important. If space permits, decorate the corners with round planters. Their size should be appropriate and should not interfere with traffic. Heavy objects can be placed on the landing, pictures or photos with landscapes and happy faces can also be hung. A staircase that is well lit and decorated with artistic pictures attracts good Chi and reinforces the movement of energy between the different stories of the house.

Exposed Beams

Beams are attractive when they are varied and arranged in a pattern. But when there are only one or two, they can be oppressive and aggressive. When two people sleep under an exposed beam that runs across the bed, it is usually causes a lack of communication. If the beam is aligned between the two, its shape projects an invisible barrier and over time can cause separation or even divorce. There are various Feng Shui decorating solutions to resolve this situation. The bed can be moved to the other side of the room, bamboo Chinese flutes or decorative fringe can be hung on the beam, or an attractive mobile can be hung to give a lifting effect.

Other effects of exposed beams:

If a beam is above the head of the bed, it can cause headaches or migraines.

Beams over the dining table or stove are a source of financial loss.

Beams above a desk or work space can affect the nervous system.

A beam in a closed area of a house or business such as an entryway can block positive Chi and interfere with circulation.

Solutions:

Hang two Chinese bamboo flutes tied with ribbons on the beam so that it forms the shape of the Ba-Gua. or attach a strip of red cloth along the beam.

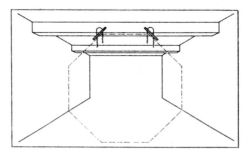

The Placement of Chinese Bamboo Flutes

When they are well placed, shapes, colors and objects help Chi to flow harmoniously throughout the house. When there are missing pieces in the layout of the home or aggressive corners that greet guests or the inhabitants of a space, we should fix the situation by changing the furniture and using traditional Feng Shui methods.

The Placement of Furniture and Electrical Appliances

When decorating spaces that have many angular shapes, try to choose furniture that is rounded and without sharp corners. If there are tables or furniture with corners, place them on the diagonal so that the corners don't point toward the entrance door or toward the seating area.

Stereo equipment, televisions and computers should be placed in the "finance" area.

Beds and desks should not be in line with the entrance nor biting it.

When a bed is located under a window, the health and mood of the person sleeping there can be affected. Hang a crystal ball or Chinese bamboo

89

flutes above it. Reinforce with the Three Secrets. (The crystal ball should be hung in the middle of the upper part of the window frame.)

Furniture should be located in the most appropriate place based on its shape, size, texture and color, making certain that it doesn't obstruct doors or cut off the flow of traffic.

Chairs and sofas should be placed away from the fireplace. Avoid blocking the door or positioning the furniture so people sitting there have their back to the door.

The Nine Minor Additions of the Tradition

The Nine Minor Additions of the tradition help create harmonious spaces. The principles of beauty are based on the essence and the quality of the change, not on size or quantity. A small detail can eliminate and harmonize a large negative situation.

1. Bright Objects

Bright objects include mirrors, Feng Shui crystal balls (20 mm, 30 mm, 40 mm, 50 mm, 60 mm, 70 mm or 80 mm in diameter) and lights.

Mirrors are the first option for balancing and solving areas with weak energy. Mirrors reflect, clarify and amplify a space.

Mirrors are used in Feng Shui both inside and outside the house. A small circular mirror with the trigrams on it is known as a Ba-Gua mirror. They are used when protection or help is required. Hang them outside in a high place, like above the main door of an establishment or house. They can also be hung high on a building pointed at an area of negative emanations.

Dark corners and hallways, and spaces with little light have poor quality Chi. Lighting in a house is very important and should be as similar to sunlight as possible. Light has a balancing effect and fills empty spaces.

2. Colors

Colors are used to reinforce the quality of Chi. White represents purity and transparency as well as the absence of life. Red is the color of luck and represents strength and joy. Red is used in ceremonies like the Chinese New Year, weddings and births. Green represents growth and vitality. Blue is close to green on the color spectrum as it moves toward black. Blue is colder than green and manifests calmness and mental tranquillity; it is a good color for studies and libraries. Black represents the depths of the ocean where light doesn't reach and with the depths of the self. It is related to career and profession and represents justice, sobriety and rectitude. Yellow is happy and attracts good luck and prosperity. It vibrates with the Chi of Earth and reinforces physical and mental health.

3. Sounds

Wind chimes and bells have been used for hundreds of years as objects of protection and warning. The chimes used in Feng Shui should have a clear and harmonious sound. When they are hung on the back door of a business or home, they bring mental harmony to those who live or work there, while also acting as an alarm system. They also help children listen to their parent's advice. The sounds of chimes and bells bring positive influence, prosperity and money.

Another sound adjustment is music. Music, like meditation and classical styles, feeds the soul and elevates the spirit of our homes and work places. Even when we leave, it is good to leave the music on as the melodious sounds harmonize the space, help plants to grow and improve pets' moods.

4. Vital Life-Force

Plants represent vital life-force, disperse Chi and help energy to flow. They help our Chi circulate and elevate the quality of Chi in within a space. Another means of increasing vital-life force is to use fish tanks.

5. Kinetic Energy

Water fountains are healthy and serve to reinforce energy. If the fountain has a cascade, it should be positioned facing the home where it will bring good luck and prosperity. Other moving objects that can be used as Feng Shui adjustments are fans, windmills, flags and watering systems. These moving systems circulate energy and fill areas that are missing or weakened by the shape of the land or house. Hanging flags in front of a property or business elevates and strengthens the energy that flows toward the site.

6. Heavy Objects

Heavy Objects such as sculptures strengthen the energy of the area where they are. A business will be strengthened by placing an artistic sculpture, representative of the business, in the career or profession area. A sculpture in the marriage area will strengthen the relationship of the couple living in the house.

7. Electrical Energy

The use of energy also includes electrical and potential energy. Electrical energy can be used to feed the power area that corresponds to the trigram «Sun.» Placing electrical appliances, computers, televisions and stereo systems in this area helps physical and spiritual abundance.

8. Symbols

Using symbols like Chinese bamboo flutes, the Ba-Gua and shapes corresponding to the elements also are part of the Minor Additions. To honor fame at your desk, you can place a crystal pyramid in the fame area. The pyramid or cone shape represents the fire element and is related to fame. The symbolism of its shape transcends the symbolism of the material it is made out of (crystal represents the water element). Using spiritual or sacred symbols in the center of the home, based on the «Yu-Nei» or sacred area, strengthens our very essence and nature. Using symbolic shapes such as an angel in the marriage or relationship area reinforces this life area or activity. Always reinforce any adjustment with the Three Secrets.

Chinese bamboo flutes are transcendental Feng Shui objects. They are used to balance walls and ceilings that are not symmetrical, exposed beams and general obstructions in the structure of a home or business. The flutes should be hung in a position that reinforces the Ba-Gua, with the mouth of the flute facing upward. Flutes symbolize peace and protection. Many businesses hang flutes close to the cash register as a security measure. After a Chinese bamboo flute has been used as a transcendental adjustment, it should never be used as a musical instrument.

9. Other Additions

Among other additions, we can mention the use of flags, curtains, incense and fragrances. A flag hung in the front of an establishment brings happiness with its movement and elevates Chi. The colors of the flag should be chosen carefully. When flags are combined with other symbols, they become much more powerful.

Decorative objects such as pictures or photographs should be hung with taste. Art work depicting angry or bitter people should be replaced with landscapes, pleasing scenery and happy people.

Rugs can also be used. A circular rug softens a room decorated with many angular shapes.

Mirrors, Flutes, Bells and Crystals in Feng Shui

So far, we have mentioned only the most common objects used in the Chinese art of placement. As Master Lin Yun states, personal will and intention determine how an object is used. It is the power and clarity of your will and intent that determines the effectiveness of the solution you choose. We will briefly explain how to use the objects we have mentioned. Intuition and imagination on your part can increase this list.

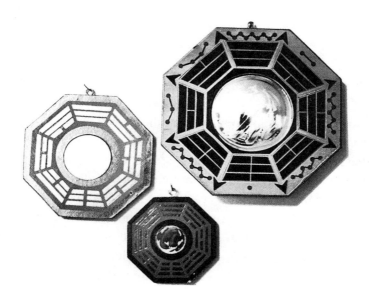

Ba-Gua Mirrors

Mirrors

Mirrors guide, direct, amplify and strengthen the flow of Chi. They attract prosperous Chi and balance a space by bringing in outside energy. In an apartment or house on the ocean, a mirror hung on an interior wall facing the water will bring water energy inside and balance the flow of Chi. Mirrors reflect and strengthen images. They allow the creative force of Chi to penetrate closed areas. The quality of the mirror is more important than its shape or size. It is important to see your face's refection in it, although they can remain hidden. When you use a mirror to deflect negative energy, have compassion.

A built-in closet at the end of a hall creates stagnant Chi. Hang a mirror on the inside wall to open and expand the space and to strengthen the flow of Chi.

Chinese Bamboo Flutes

The power of bamboo gives strength and support. A bamboo flute is a symbol of peace and protection and elevates vital life-force. The size of the flute affects its power.

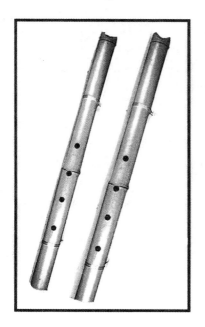

Chinese Bamboo Flutes

Bells and Wind Chimes

The highest level of music is the music of spheres. It is projected throughout the Universe and reflected in nature. Our very being is pleased when we hear the music made by the wind flowing through tree branches and prairie grass, the murmur of ocean waves, the water in a brook or the song of a bird.

Use bells to awaken or clear your mind. Their sound captures your attention so you are open to receiving subtle impressions. Their shape and sound have the power to raise ceilings or low-hanging eaves. They raise Chi, elevate weakened or depressed energy, increase fame and reputation, bring good luck, open up enclosed areas, harmonize Chi within a space and strengthen communication among family members and people in the work place. When buying a bells or wind chimes, their sound quality is the most important factor. Bells should be placed based on their size and function. Bells and wind chimes affect the flow of Chi even when they are not in motion.

Crystals

According to Master Ni Hua Ching, «The true mind is the balanced mind. The true mind is the integrated mind. The true mind is the mind as transparent as crystal.»

Use crystals to balance and adjust the flow of Chi near doors, windows or vestibules. They can be used to balance conflictive situations when beds or desks are aligned with doors. Crystals can be used in place of bells, wind chimes or mirrors. They refract and reflect sunlight as well as spiritual and universal light. They are windows that connect our internal consciousness with our light messengers and our angels. Crystals reflect a message of light even when they are hung in dark spaces or corners. A crystal hung behind a curtain, still has the same effect as if it were hung in sight.

External and Internal Circumstances
Can Cause Problems in Different Life Areas

The following are some more common situations that can create conflict in each of the nine life areas of the Ba-Gua.

Fame

Exterior:

Adjacent buildings, their physical state and Chi of their inhabitants.
Aggressive corners of adjacent buildings.
«T» intersections.

Streets or rivers that curve away from the right side of the house.

A plot of land that is narrower in back than in front.

Garages in front of the house.

A lake, canal or river behind the house.

The fame area missing in the house or property.

Interior:

Front door blocked by trees, columns or walls.

The front door hidden or on the side of the house.

The front door in line with a corner of the property (diamond shaped plot).

Bathroom located above the front door.

Bathroom in the fame area.

Windows blocked by trees.

Windows that open up and down instead of out.

Built-in closet or extra «junk» room in the fame area.

Mechanical or electrical systems that aren't working properly.

The bed in line with the entrance door of the room.

A bed surrounded by doors.

A bed in the center of the room.

The bed in line with an aggressive corner (wall or column).

A bed without a view of the door.

(Desks or offices are subject to the same principles as the location of beds.)

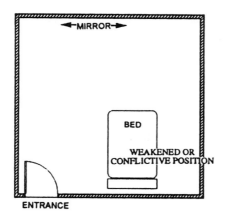

SOLUTION: MOVE THE BED TO THE COMMAND POSITION. IF THIS IS NOT POSSIBLE, HANG A MIRROR THAT GIVES A VIEW OF THE DOOR.

97

Personal Relationships and Marriage

Exterior:

> Land plot with unequal sides.
> A house at the end of a dead-end street.
> Front door below street level.
> Missing piece in the marriage area of the house or property.

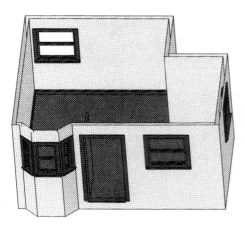

HOUSE

MISSING PIECE IN MARRIAGE AREA. COLORS CAN BE USED AS A CURE IN A MISSING AREA. PLACE PLANTS WITH PINK FLOWERS, OR PAINT THE WALL PINK, WHITE OR RED.

FRONT DOOR

Interior:

> Office in the marriage area.
> Additions in the marriage area that are not connected to the house.
> Bathroom in the marriage area.
> Split view at the front door.
> Staircase biting the front door.
> Doors (adult voices) that don't line up.
> Master bedroom with many doors.
> A doorway without a door between the master bedroom and bath.
> A beam along the bed.
> Kitchen located in an addition to the marriage area.

Children and Creativity

Exterior:

Neighboring houses with aggressive roofs or walls that point toward the children area of the home.

A house located in a forked intersection.

A house located in a «V» intersection.

Front door on a corner (triangular shaped property).

A corner of the pool pointing at the main bedroom.

Missing children area in the house or property.

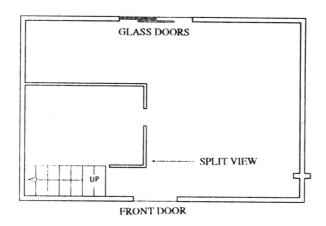

Interior:

Wall, staircase or column pointing at or splitting the front door.

Bathroom facing the front door.

Children's room above the garage or in the basement.

Children's room in line with the front door.

Beam above the child's bed or desk.

Fireplace in the children area.

Kitchen in the children area.

Mirrors that cut off the view of the head.

Size or number of windows not in balance with the doors.

Windows that are broken or don't open properly.

Windows that are blocked.

Double front doors that open out.

Closet or extra «junk» room in disorder, especially in the children's area.

Benefactors

Exterior:

> Entrance path narrower than the front door.
> Missing piece in the benefactors area.

Interior:

> Front door blocked.
> Front door hidden.
> Kitchen that can be seen from the front door.
> Kitchen too close to the front door.
> Guest room in the power position of the house.
> Noisy or broken doors and windows.
> Too many doors.
> Bed located under a window.
> Bed without a headboard.
> Desk with its seating position to a window.
> Seating area in line with the front door and the patio doors.
> Furniture obstructing the front door.
> Dining table in line with the front door and the back door.

Career and Profession

Exterior:

> Front door below street level.
> Buildings with aggressive corners facing a house.
> House built in the front part of the land plot.
> A hill or mountain in front of the house.
> House built on a forked intersection.
> Front door in the center of a «U» shaped house.
> View from the front door blocked.
> Square columns in front of the house.
> Missing piece in the career and profession area of the house or property.

Interior:

> Stove top visible front the front door.
> Bathroom above the front door.
> Square columns inside the house.
> Ceilings of varying levels.
> Desk or office under a slanted ceiling or a beam.

Desk or office surrounded by doors.

A desk that is too small or too large.

Bathroom on the floor above a desk or office.

Kitchen in the front of the house.

Fireplace in the front of the house.

Warped or uneven floors.

Knowledge

Exterior:

Corner of a building pointing at the knowledge area.

Blocked windows in the knowledge area.

Missing piece in the knowledge area.

Entrance below street level.

Interior:

Narrow entrance.

Beams in the bedroom or study.

Slanted ceilings.

Desk under a slanted ceiling or beams.

Desk in line with the door.

Many doors in the bedrooms or study.

Broken wina ws and screens.

Broken mirrors.

Family

Exterior:

Street or bridge aligned with the house.

Buildings with aggressive corners.

Streets, rivers or canals that curve away from the right side of the house.

Front door below street level.

House located on a «V» intersection.

A land plot that is narrower in back than in front.

Corner of the pool points toward the family area.

House on top of a mountain.

Missing piece in the family area of the house or property.

Narrow entrance.

Front door blocked by trees, square columns or walls.

A triangular shaped land plot, with the entrance on the corner.

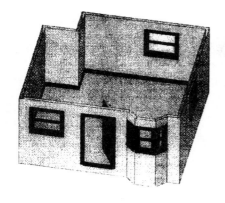

HOUSE

MISSING PIECE IN THE FINANCES AREA. COLORS CAN BE USED AS A CURE FOR THIS AREA. PLACE PLANTS WITH PURPLE FLOWERS. PAINT THE WALL PURPLE; OR GREEN, PURPLE AND RED.

Interior:

Bathroom in the center of the house.

Bathroom facing the kitchen.

Bathroom opposite the front door.

Front door in line with the back patio door.

No back door, especially if it is a business.

Conflictive doors, doors that don't talk.

Back door in the family area.

Stairs facing the front door.

Beam above the stove or over the dining table.

Blocked hallways.

A microwave above (pressuring) the stove top.

Kitchen in an addition to the family area.

Cook with his/her back to the entrance of the kitchen.

Stove top in the corner of the kitchen.

Broken or unused burners.

Kitchen in line with a toilet on the other side of the wall.

Kitchen, bed or office on the lower edge of a "boot" shaped room or house.

Bed in line with a toilet on the other side of the wall.

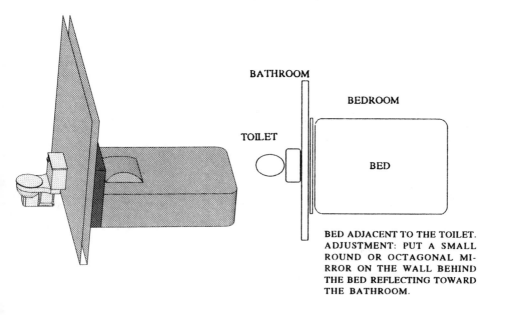

BATHROOM

BEDROOM

TOILET

BED

BED ADJACENT TO THE TOILET.
ADJUSTMENT: PUT A SMALL
ROUND OR OCTAGONAL MI-
RROR ON THE WALL BEHIND
THE BED REFLECTING TOWARD
THE BATHROOM.

Physical and Mental Health

Exterior:

House facing a cemetery or funeral home.

Neighboring buildings with aggressive corners.

House facing a T intersection.

House facing a hill or mountain.

Streets, rivers or canals that curve away from the front or right side of the house.

Dry plants or dead trees in front of the house.

Trees or columns blocking the front door.

Corner of the pool pointing at the house.

Interior:

Bathroom in the center of the house.

Bathroom in view of the front door.

Bathroom or kitchen located on the central line of the house.

Bathroom located above the kitchen, especially if the toilet is above the stove.

Bathroom at the end of a long hall.

Bathroom opposite the front door, even if it is not seen.

Bathroom above a bedroom, especially if the toilet is above the bed.

Two bathroom doors that hit.

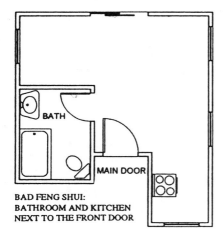

BAD FENG SHUI:
BATHROOM AND KITCHEN
NEXT TO THE FRONT DOOR

BATH

MAIN DOOR

RECOMMENDATIONS:
1 - HANG A MIRROR ON THE BATHROOM DOOR, SEAL THE BATHROOM OR HANG A FENG SHUI CRYSTAL BALL.
2 - HANG A MIRROR ON THE WALL BEHIND THE STOVE. REINFORCE WITH THE THREE SECRETS.

Bathroom next to the front door.

Master bedroom visible from the front door.

Bedroom over the garage.

Kitchen next to the front door.

Kitchen in the center of the house.

Fireplace in the center of the house.

Stove top visible from the main entrance.

Blocked doors.

Doors that hit or that aren't aligned.

Front door aligned with the back patio door.

Many doors in a small room.

Spiral staircase in the center of the home.

Narrow stairs.

Slanted ceilings.

Low ceilings.

Beams over the bed or dining table.

Broken or blocked windows.

Mechanical or electrical systems that don't work properly.
Unbalanced colors.
Bed under a window.
Bed without space, circulation between the mattress and the ground.
Bed opposite the stove top or toilet on the other side of the wall.
Desk with its back to the door.
Beds and desks under beams or near columns.
Mirrors that cut off the view of your head.
Furniture close to the fireplace.

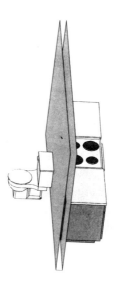

TOILET ADJACENT
TO THE STOVE.

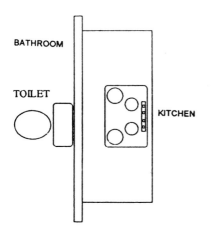

BATHROOM

TOILET

KITCHEN

STOVE AND TOILET ARE IN
CONFLICT.
ADJUSTMENT:
HANG A MIRROR BEHIND THE
STOVE TOP TO REFLECT THE
BURNERS; HANG A SMALL BELL
ABOVE THE PLACE WHERE THE
PERSON WHO COOKS STANDS.

Finances, Physical and Spiritual Abundance

Exterior:

> Land plot with unequal sides.
>
> Land plot wider in front than back.
>
> Water behind the house (lake, river, pool), very detrimental if it is a bay.
>
> Street that curves away from the property in the finances area.
>
> House at the end of a dead-end street or cul-de-sac.
>
> Missing piece in the career and profession area.
>
> Missing piece in the finances area.
>
> Conflict in the finances area: aggressive buildings in the finances area.
>
> Water draining from the roof or outdoor faucet toward the street, dry or scant vegetation in the finances area.

Interior:

> Bathroom in the finances area.
>
> Split wall at the entrance to the finances area.
>
> Secret arrows (corners of columns or walls) in the finances area.
>
> Broken doors or windows in the finances area.
>
> Water leaking in the finances area.
>
> Bad plumbing in the finances area.
>
> Stairs in the finances area.
>
> Stairs biting the front door, located in the career and profession area.

III

TRANSCENDENTAL SOLUTIONS

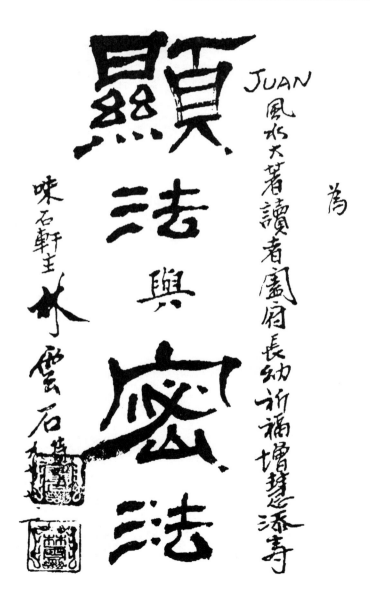

Feng Shui makes us aware of both visible and invisible factors that influence a space. It guides us through its art, philosophy, principles and methods to balance these factors and create harmonious relationships within the space and with those who live there. The Black Hat Tantric Tibetan School of Feng Shui focuses on the following points:

1. Visible factors.
2. Invisible factors.
3. Use of visible solutions of the tradition.
4. Use of transcendental, Tantric Tibetan Buddhist solutions.
5. Concentration of Yin energy. Establishing a connection with the energy of the space.
6. Emphasis on transcendental solutions. Using Tibetan methods such as Tracing the Nine Stars, the Dharma Wheel* and others.

The visible Feng Shui solutions (Yang) should be accompanied by a sacred intention to honor the manifestation of the divine through the trigrams of the Ba-Gua (Yin).

Visible Solutions of the Tradition

The visible solutions are made up of the Principles and the Nine Minor Additions of the tradition.

---

* The Dharma Wheel is the most divine, Tibetan meditation that consists of walking through the house reciting Om Ma Ni Pad Me Hum.

The Nine Minor Additions:

1. Bright object. Lamps, candles, Feng Shui crystal balls and other bright objects.
2. Colors. Use of fabric, pictures, natural or artificial flowers.
3. Sound. Bells, wind chimes, music.
4. Live elements. Bonsai, plants, fish tanks, others.
5. Kinetic energy. Water, wind mills, flags, water fountains.
6. Heavy objects. Statues, rocks and others.
7. Electrical energy. Objects that run on electricity.
8. Symbols. Pyramids, sacred symbols, Chinese bamboo flutes, the Ba-Gua and Chinese coins.

The visible solutions or Minor Additions of the tradition should be reinforced with the Three Secrets.

Principles of the Tradition

The Principles of the tradition are practical suggestions to be used at home, the office, or in businesses. See page 42 .

The Transcendental Method

The art of placement of Feng Shui has two aspects. The external aspect (Yang) is aesthetic and based on the shapes, colors and design of the areas following the fundamental principles of Feng Shui. The internal aspect (Yin), or transcendental method, depends on the preparation and intentions of the student or practitioner.

The external aspect of Feng Shui includes information about how the Ba-Gua is applied to a piece of property, house or office to determine the lines of harmony. The principles of the tradition can also be used to reinforce areas weakened by angular and aggressive shapes, exposed beams, split views, or by a layout that is conducive to stagnant Chi. Decorating using the principles of the external aspect of Feng Shui will help achieve favorable results between 20% and 30%.

The transcendental method is different. The practitioner who uses the transcendental method of Feng Shui decoration will achieve favorable results of 120% in whatever area needs attention. The results will always depend on the understanding and intention of the practitioner. Those who wish to use the transcendental method should receive oral instruction directly from Master Thomas Lin Yun by attending one of his seminars, or from one of his students. After having received this teaching and dedicated time to studying and practicing the theory and philosophy of Feng Shui, we should then ask ourselves the following questions:

1. Am I ready to use the transcendental method?

    If a practitioner or professional wants to include this method in her work, this question becomes very important. Before using it, the practitioner must prepare herself very carefully. Her Chi should be reinforced with meditation so that she can successfully transmute negative energy and emotions into light, harmony and prosperity. She should familiarize herself with the method to be used and be very careful to harmonize her Chi before doing a transcendental cure. This preparation is done through prayer and meditation.

2. Can I use the transcendental method?

    If a person lives alone, they can ask and answer this question themselves. If a family is involved, they should be told before hand what Feng Shui, and especially the transcendental method, is. A Feng Shui practitioner should respect the privacy of those who have hired him to design or decorate their space. Before using the transcendental method, you must always ask permission first, and then should explain what is involved. If the person is open to it, the practitioner can proceed with the appropriate method. The «tradition of the red envelope» should also be explained. The red envelope has a special place in Feng Shui. It is how we honor the masters who have given us this knowledge. Honoring the tradition of the red envelope allows the transcendental method to be used with results of 120%. The practitioner should explain the use of the red envelope and after having received one, should sleep with it placed in his pillowcase that same night. Red envelopes, similar to the ones found in the back of this book can be purchased at any bazaar or store with Chinese artifacts.

3. Should I use it now?

This third question is the most important. After answering the first two, we must also make sure that the energy of the space is right for us to use a transcendental method at this moment. We must question the energy of the space and feel the answer with our hearts. If it is not the right time, we must wait. The transcendental methods are used to reinforce the visible changes made in Feng Shui decoration. Sometimes, the transcendental method is the only way to harmonize a conflictive area. For example, a column blocking the front door has a restrictive and blocking effect at the Mouth of Chi. This affects the prosperity of those who live or work in the space. The solution is to use a transcendental method.

When the practitioner decides to use a transcendental method, he must follow the ethics of his profession and the suggestions of the tradition. Before beginning a transcendental method, some type of meditation should be done. Although the tradition suggests using the Sun Meditation to the Buddha, any other type of meditation, in keeping with the practitioner's religious belief, is equally as valid.

The following are some transcendental methods:

1. The Three Secrets
2. The movement of the eight trigrams.
3. Tracing the Nine Star Path.
4. The Wheel of the Eight Doors.
5. Exterior adjustment of Chi.
6. Interior adjustment of Chi.
7. Others.

112

THE THREE SECRETS

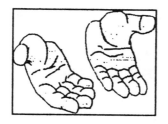

1-mudra

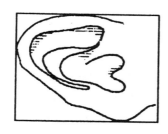

2-mantra

3-sutra

The Three Secrets

This mystical ritual reinforces whatever solution has been chosen as well any other ritual that has been previously used. The ritual of the Three Secrets combines three elements: body, speech and mind.

1. Body. The ritual of the body uses gestures or mudras -concrete hand or body positions. Shaking hands is an example of a mudra that expresses feelings of friendship. The Peace Mudra is a hand position that calms the heart and mind. This mudra is done by placing the left hand over the right with the palms facing up. The thumbs should be lightly touching each other. The hands are then positioned at the height of the solar plexus.

The Peace Mudra

2. Speech. The power of the word in mantras strengthens the essence of the emanations of Chi. The most common mantras are: The Six True Words: Om Ma Ni Pad Me Hum and the Heart Mantra: Cate-Cate, Poro-Cate, Poro-Som-Cate, Bode-Soha.
3. Mind. More importantly than either the mudras or the mantras is the mind. The state of consciousness, the sincere intention and the purity of thought, is what establishes the intimate contact with the creative force of Chi.

Other mudras (body and hand positions) and mantras can be used. Another mudra is the Expelling Mudra. This is done by joining the middle and ring finger with the thumb. When the thumb is supporting the two fingers, flick open while reciting the mantra of the Six True Words: Om Man Ni Pad Me Hum. Men should do it with the left hand, women with their right.

All objects that are used to balance a life area of the Ba-Gua should be reinforced with the Three Secrets. When a mirror is hung on a bathroom door because its water element (water that drains) is in conflict with the line of fire where it is located, the mirror should be reinforced with the Three Secrets. When we place a live plant, one of the Minor Additions of the tradition, to reinforce a specific activity in our lives, we should always add our intention using the Three Secrets.

Feng Shui is done step by step. A home or work place is a Universe of energies. Chi is reflected through shapes, colors and the energies present. We might imagine that this Universe of energies is like a giant tree of light with branches, leaves, fruit, trunk and roots. The energy tree must be kept in good condition. Feng Shui is environmental acupuncture. The student and practitioner reinforce weak areas and balance the positive and negative manifestations to create the unity of the Tao.

For better results using the transcendental method, we should use them during the most favorable times of the day according to Chinese astrology.

After having studied the space and decided the methods to be used, it should be sealed by Tracing the Nine Star Path.

When there are situations that require special attention, we can use other transcendental methods.

All transcendental methods should be sealed by using red envelopes.

Tracing the Nine Star Path

This is the most important adjustment for cleansing the home and harmonizing it with blessings.

Recite the Heart Mantra nine times: Cate-Cate, Poro-Cate, Poro-Som-Cate, Bode-Soha. Visualize your body radiating light. Move through the house, physically or mentally, according the Ba-Gua as follows:

1. Family - Green   Jupiter
2. Money - Purple   Polar Star
3. Health - Yellow   Saturn
4. Friends - Gray   Sun
5. Children - White   Venus
6. Knowledge - Blue   The star, Deneb
7. Fame - Red   Mars
8. Career - Black   Mercury
9. Marriage - Pink   Moon

As you move through each of the nine areas, use the Three Secrets: the mudra position, the correct mental attitude and the Heart Mantra.

- Recite the Heart Mantra (Cate-Cate, Poro-Cate, Poro-Som-Cate, Bode-Soha).
- Visualize your body infused with ten thousand lights.
- Move physically or mentally through the nine stars projecting the light that is coming from inside you to the walls, floor, ceiling and furniture.

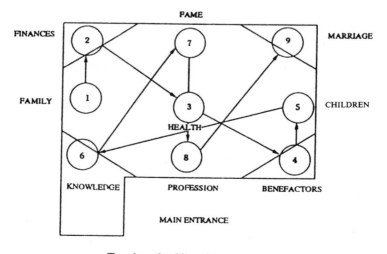

Tracing the Nine Stars

This is a personal exercise that strengthens Chi and eliminates any type of negativity.

The Wheel of the Eight Doors

Another method for adjusting Chi is known as the "Wheel of Eight Doors." Two octagonal wheels, one fixed and the other constantly rotating around the center are visualized. The moving wheel rotates with eight life situations in the following order: life, accident, imagination, experience, death, fear, possibility and rest. Of these situations, life is the most desirable and death the least. Rest signifies allowing things to just happen which could mean that negative events could perhaps change into positive events. Imagination is linked with the creative faculty where negative elements are transformed into positive ones, bad into good. The adjustment involves bringing life to all the situations, transforming everything into the energy of light, life and love.

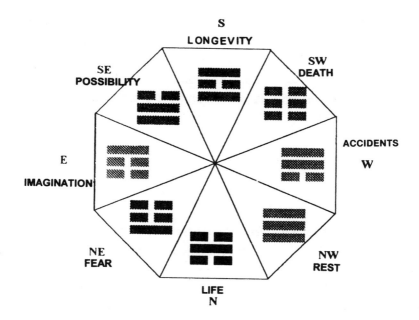

Imagine two octagons, one fixed and the other rotating. When you enter the door to a house or room, try to feel which of the eight life situations meets you as you reach the threshold. Before taking the first step, feel the energy of the octagon. If the life situation is positive, take the step. Then visualize the other situations and move them toward the door where «life» is found. Another way to bring «life» to these situations is to Trace the Nine Star Path. Visualize that «life» moves to the family area of the Ba-Gua and begin Tracing the Nine Stars. Bring light, life and love to all the situations in the octagon through the trigrams of the Ba-Gua.

Adjusting External Chi

Adjusting the External Chi or "Yu Wai" is a ritual that produces a prosperous rebirth in the space. Hold a handful of rice in your palm and reinforce it with the Three Secrets. Sprinkle it around interior perimeter of the building or apartment, then empty the rest outside the house, apartment or building. Outside, in the corners of the building or property, throw three handfuls of rice in the air visualizing that it is feeding all the negative spirits so they will leave the vicinity. Then throw three handfuls to Earth visualizing that the energies of prosperity, happiness and health are awakening. Reinforce each position with the Three Secrets.

Adjusting Internal Chi

When the shape of a house or apartment is symmetrical, you can use the transcendental «Yu-Nei» method or adjustment of the Internal Chi. Draw a floor plan of the house, apartment or room. Draw lines to connect the opposite corners. Then connect each corner to the center point of the opposite wall. The intersection of the lines will create a central space that is special and sacred. Place a heavy object or live plant here. Reinforce it with the Three Secrets.

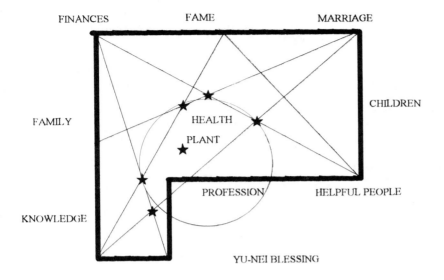

FINANCES   FAME   MARRIAGE

CHILDREN

FAMILY   HEALTH

PLANT

KNOWLEDGE

PROFESSION   HELPFUL PEOPLE

YU-NEI BLESSING

The Tradition of the Red Envelope

Each time that Feng Shui information is shared, we should honor the tradition. The exchange of energy between the person who gives the information and the person who receives it is sealed with the red envelope. The red envelopes should be new. When the information is given over the phone, the red envelope must be received first.

The number of red envelopes is decided based on the importance of the information and the number of recommendations. For each recommendation, ask for 1, 3, 9, 27, 99, or 108 red envelopes. Each envelope should have some money inside.

The numbers 1, 3, and 9 symbolize unity, creation and complete manifestation.

In giving the information, you should keep in mind the need and sincerity of the person asking for it. If someone needs Feng Shui information, they must ask for it. The person requesting information should give a red envelope before receiving the information.

The red envelope seals the information shared and shows respect for the tradition and for the sacred work of the Masters who shared secrets of Heaven and Earth about protecting Chi.

When receiving red envelopes, you should sleep with them under your pillow that night having first done the Three Secrets. The next morning the contents can be donated or used for some Feng Shui need.

At the end of this book, you will find a red envelope. If you wish to use a transcendental method, you should honor the tradition of the red envelope. Mail it with a donation to the Temple of Lin Yun, 2959 Russell Street, Berkeley CA, 94705, USA.

Transcendental Solutions
(Recommended by Master Lin Yun)

Transcendental solutions may cause controversy with some people, as they may seem irrational, illogical, or even superstitious. However, we must remember that there are regions in the Universe where transcendental solutions have their own logic and are accepted by most of the inhabitants. To obtain better results for our Feng Shui changes, we should use transcendental logic and suspend our judgment of what goes beyond the limits of our knowledge. In reality, this knowledge is inside us and if we look deep within, past our five senses we will find the mystical truth of the transcendental solution.

The reality of the Universe that we perceive through our senses represents a logical system. When we use a method that transcends logical understanding of the laws of physics, some people begin to worry. We must remember that the physical Universe, with its laws and logical viewpoint, is born and nurtured from an essence that comes from an illogical region whose source is in the unmanifested, nonexistent and illogical which is the divine essence of the spirit.

The following are some transcendental solutions from Master Thomas Lin Yun that may help with different problems.

Transcendental Solution to Sell a House

The best time to use this method is between 11 a.m. and 1 p.m. It can also be done during the person's favorable hours based on Chinese astrology.

Method:

1. Between 11 a.m. and 1 p.m., take a small object from the kitchen or from the house's foundation such as a door handle, a screw or piece of brick, etc... (It can also be done during the person's favorable hours based on Chinese astrology.)
2. During the time mentioned above (if possible) go to a place with flowing water (a river, brook or ocean).
3. Throw the object in the water.
4. Visualize the object and the new owner, happy and pleased, both moving with the current and making the move. Feel the house change hands.
7. You can reflect on any type of tie that you have to the house. Take a moment and listen closely. This can be a time of great clarity. Perhaps you will see changes that should be made to the house to improve its appearance.
8. Reinforce it with the Three Secrets.
9. Leave without looking back.

Important:

Don't mention this transcendental method to anyone until the house has been sold.

Replace the object after the house has been sold and before the new owner gets the key.

You can use the Blessing Mudra to weaken whatever obstacle is slowing the sale of the house.

If you share this or any of the following information with others, you must honor the tradition of the red envelope.

Conceiving a Child - Transcendental Method

This ritual should be done when a couple wishes to have a baby. The following items are needed:

1. Nine lotus seeds
2. Nine peanuts
3. Nine dried dates
4. Nine lichi nuts
5. A bowl

Follow these steps:

1. Place the seeds, dates and nuts in the bowl and fill it three-quarters of the way with water.
2. Before going to sleep, place the bowl outside so it is exposed to the heavens. Invite the creative force of God to infuse the water in the bowl and the house. Visualize that the Virgin brings a you a healthy baby.
3. Place the bowl under the bed directly in line with the abdomen of the woman.
4. Reinforce with the Three Secrets.
5. Every morning for nine days, change the water and leave it outside, inviting the creative force of God into the house.
6. After nine days, pour the water on a plant and bury the seeds, dates and nuts in the dirt.
7. Place the plant near the front door, either inside or out, and reinforce with the Three Secrets.
8. Repeat the process for two more days using two additional plants.
9. Place the second plant in the living room near the entrance and the third in the master bedroom in the children area. Do not move the bed or clean under it during this time.

A. Mental Clarity

1. Get two round mirrors between 7 and 9 cm in diameter.
2. Place one of the mirrors in the sun for a total of 12 hours and place the other in the moon light for a total of 12 hours.

3. Glue the two mirrors together, back to back, and put then under your pillow and sleep with them for 27 nights.
4. Each morning repeat the Heart Mantra nine times. (Cate-Cate, Poro-Cate, Poro-Som-Cate, Bode-Soha) Then clean the mirror while visualizing that you are cleaning away your problems.
5. Reinforce with the Three Secrets:
   a. Peace Mudra
   b. Mantra: (Cate-Cate, Poro-Cate, Poro-Som-Cate, Bode-Soha.)
   c. Visualize mental clarity. Repeat the Six True Words nine times: Om Ma Ni Pad Me Hum.
6. Lastly, perform the Expelling Mudra.

B. Fulfillment

1. Practice the breathing technique that follows while remaining conscious of breathing in healthy, creative life force from the Universe, and exhaling any negative energy you have been holding in your body, or problem that has been bothering you.
2. Inhale deeply. Exhale through your mouth eight times as if you were blowing it out. On the ninth time, the exhalation should be long, getting rid of the remaining oxygen.
3. Practice this exercise 9 consecutive times each day for 9 or 27 consecutive days.

C. Creation

1. For 9 or 27 days, meet 9 new people. Don't judge or speak poorly of anyone. Maintain positive thoughts.
2. Do this for 9 or 27 days.

Six True Words Exercise

1. Take a deep breath, filling the lungs. Exhale in nine parts, making the last exhalation the longest.
2. Take a deep breath, visualize the Six True Words Mantra (Om Man Ni Pad Me Hum) with the respective colors of the mantra in each corresponding part of the body.
3. Repeat the Six True Words Mantra 3 times.

This exercise can be used when a person is tired and energy levels are low.

The Three Harmonies

The three harmonies is one the most advanced methods using the lines of harmony of the Ba-Gua. They represent the lines of a triangle and are based on the harmonic relations between trines.

The Transcendental Method of the Four Red Ribbons to Protect a Marriage

This method is an example of the three harmonies. If your marriage is going through difficult times due to arguments and differing of opinions, you can use the four red ribbons transcendental method. Get a meter-long red ribbon and cut it into four, 25 cm pieces. Glue each ribbon on the upper part of the symbol of a Ba-Gua mirror in the following trigrams: 1) Ch'ien (benefactors) 2) Khan (career and profession) 3) Chen (family) and 4) Sun (finances).

When you glue each ribbon, reinforce it with the Three Secrets.

Hang the Ba-Gua in the marriage area; it doesn't have to be seen.

This method can be used for the rest of the areas of the Ba-Gua as well.

All the trigrams of the Ba-Gua resonate through trines or aspects of the three harmonies. The figure of the three harmonies shows four triangles. Their sides connect the trigrams that are related. This relationship implies that when a negative condition, weakness or conflict exists in an area, it can be helped with intention, adjustments and arrangements in the areas connected to it by the three harmonies.

The marriage area (Kun) receives help through the three harmonies from the benefactors area (Ch'ien), career and profession (Khan) and family (Chen).

This also implies that if there are problems in these areas (benefactors, profession and family) which aren't taken care, they could affect personal or marital relationships.

The correspondences of the trigrams, in relation with the three harmonies, are the following:

TRIGRAM	CORRESPONDENCES WITH THE 3 HARMONIES
MARRIAGE:	Benefactors, profession, family and finances
CHILDREN:	Knowledge and finances (hang 2 ribbons per trigram)
BENEFACTORS:	Knowledge, family, fame and marriage
PROFESSION:	Finances and marriage (2 ribbons per trigram)
KNOWLEDGE:	Finances, fame, children and benefactors
FAMILY:	Marriage and benefactors (2 ribbons per trigram)
FINANCES:	Marriage, children, profession and knowledge
FAME:	Benefactors and knowledge (2 ribbons per trigram)

Sealing the Doors

This transcendental method is used when moving into a space that has been previously occupied to cleanse the space of emanations and situations of negative and unknown origin. It should be used when moving into a house or business with an unknown or negative history.

To seal the seven doors, you need cinnabar (ju-sha), 150 proof liquor and a small glass bowl.

Add the cinnabar to the bowl and with an eye dropper add 99 (or your age plus one) drops of the liquor. As each drop falls, say the Six True Words Mantra. Then mix it -men with the middle finger on the right hand and women with the middle finger of the left hand.

As you are mixing it, say the Six True Words Mantra.

Take the bowl with the mixture and mark all the doors in the house on the inside. The mark should be done with the middle finger that has been dipped in the mixture. Each door should be marked with one dot in the upper center and with three dots on the side where the door opens. Mark all the doors including the front door, each room door and the garage door. Reinforce each mark with the Three Secrets and the Expelling Mudra. Women should mark the door with the middle finger of the left hand while doing the mudra with their right. Men mark with the middle finger of the right hand and do the mudra with their left. Also, mark the center underneath beds and desks as well as the areas that correspond to fame, health and profession. In the kitchen, mark the center of each burner.

The Heart Sutra Meditation

This meditation elevates and strengthens Chi and harmonizes the body's rhythms for physical and mental health. You can do it seated or lying on a bed. Use the Heart Mudra and say the Heart Sutra (Cate-Cate, Poro-Cate, Poro-Som-Cate, Bode-Soha) nine times.

Imagine absolute silence. In the distance, you begin to hear a sound that slowly comes closer. The sound is like a humming that gets louder little by little. As it becomes more audible, visualize a small, vibrant and luminous, white sphere emitting the sound. The sphere stops at your «dan tien» (about seven cm under your belly button). It begins to rotate horizontally around your body in a clockwise direction, making a total of nine rotations. Then it begins to spiral around your body toward your head, and continues back down your spinal column to the «dan tien.» After stopping there, it rotates three times around your body, horizontally. As it is going around, the white light begins to change colors. As it moves toward your third eye, it changes to red, then orange, yellow, green, blue, indigo and violet. When it reaches your third eye, the violet ball of light resonates with the energy of your being and begins to change color from violet to indigo to blue, to green, yellow, orange and finally red.

Visualize your Chi leaving your body and merging with the red ball of light. The ball begins distancing itself with your Chi and rises, journeying toward the infinite Universe, toward the presence of a superior spiritual entity. When your energy is in front of this divine presence say the Six True Word Mantra to purify your light. Visualize the light sphere entering the third eye of this divinity (Christ, Buddha, God) and into profound eternal love. Imagine that the Chi expands toward the infinite body of light so that your Chi and the light of the divine being merge into the same light. Feel one with God. Feel infinite compassion, eternal knowledge and love invade your consciousness. It is one and the same essence. Visualize the sensation of fire burning your eyes, nose, ears, tongue and whole body. Nothing remains except the your light body. Visualize an eight-petal lotus opening in your heart. In the center of the lotus are two lights, one red the other white. Under your feet, there are two lotus flowers; you find yourself seated in one with eight petals. The red light is in your heart while the white light radiates light throughout your body. Visualize the white light radiating from your body into the whole Universe, toward every dimension and the six kingdoms of beings. (The six kingdoms are: Heaven, the kingdom of the jealous gods, human beings, animals, hungry ghosts and hell.) As the light becomes more transparent and pure, it liberates the ties and suffering of all those beings who are afflicted so that they can radiate the infinite light of knowledge and love that you are reflecting. Send infinite light and blessings to all your family members, friends and neighbors wherever they may be. Send infinite light to all beings and animals in the Universe. End the meditation with the Heart Mudra and Mantra, repeating it nine times.

Sun Buddha Meditation

This is an excellent, basic meditation for adjusting your Chi before doing Feng Shui work and for achieving health and abundance. Your life will improve as you lighten the load of your daily worries, problems and tension, using light to cleanse the shadows of restriction and pressure you feel from family, friends and society.

1. Position: face the sun standing with your arms up above your head, palms facing up. Your head should be straight and feet separated.
2. Visualize the sun's light entering your body through three points: the center of your forehead, and each of the palms of your hands. Feel the sun's light moving through your entire body and leaving through the bottom of your feet. Breathe deeply and say the Six True Words Mantra nine times. Repeat this step three times.
3. Visualize the sun's light entering again through these same three points, forehead and palms. The light moves as in step two, but when it reaches your feet, it returns upward, through your whole body and leaves through the same three points, projecting back toward the

sun. Breathe deeply and say the Six True Words Mantra. Repeat this step three times.

4. Visualize the sun's light penetrating you forehead and palms again. The sun's warm and calming light moves through your whole body to your feet. When it reaches them, it begins to circle upward in a clockwise spiral. The movement is similar to going up a spiral staircase. As it moves in this spiral motion, visualize that the sun's light surrounds each of your cells, capillaries, veins, tissues, bones, muscles and organs. Feel the light and the heat of the sun cleanse your whole body, alleviating any sickness. Visualize that the spiral of light leaves through your forehead and palms toward the sun. Breathe deeply and say the Six True Words Mantra. Repeat this step three times.

Note: If you need to, rest your arms between these steps.

For best results, repeat this meditation nine times a day for nine days.

Prosperity Exercise

Many people have difficulty establishing a comfortable financial life. They have worked for years without finding the means to save enough. Each week brings expenditures that are greater than their income. Week after week, month after month, year after year, they are unable to establish a solid economic foundation. Sometimes they save some money, but then some unexpected expense depletes their savings.

Over time they program themselves to this cycle and through their own attitude, block prosperity from flowing into their lives. This barrier intensifies as the days pass.

The following exercise clears the mind and reinforces activities related to finances. It can be done to address financial difficulties and to reach a better economic situation.

One of the universal principles taught in Feng Shui is that you must learn to pay yourself before paying others.

Materials needed:

A square piece of red material, 30 cm by 30 cm.

Two circular mirrors 20 cm in diameter.

A piece of red paper between 10 and 15 cm in diameter.

A black pen that has never been used.

A bank or a glass jar with a slot in the top.

Initial preparation:

Breathe deeply and write on one side of the paper with the black pen: «Treasure Chest.»

Exhale and after inhaling again, write your name on the other side of the paper.

Stick the paper to the side of the jar with «Treasure Chest» facing out.

Daily exercise:

Select one denomination of coin.

Each day, for 27 days, separate all the coins of that denomination and do not spend them.

Each night before going to bed, deposit the coins in the Treasure Chest.

Location of the Treasure Chest:

The Treasure Chest should be placed under the bed where you sleep, aligned with your hands when your arms are by your sides.

The Treasure Chest should be placed as follows:

1. One mirror facing up.
2. The red cloth should go over the mirror.
3. Then place the Treasure Chest on top.
4. The other mirror should be placed on top, facing down.

The Treasure Chest is between the two mirrors with the bottom mirror covered by the red cloth.

This exercise should be done for 27 consecutive days. If you forget to put your coins in one day, you must start the exercise from the beginning. If you start over, it is a good idea to buy a new jar and use a new black pen to rewrite your name and «Treasure Chest» on red paper. You can use the same mirrors and red cloth.

Each day, after depositing the coins, reinforce it with the Three Secrets.

If there is a day when you don't receive any of that denomination coin, do the exercises of the Three Secrets and continue the next day.

At the end of 27 days:

You can take all the materials out from under the bed, but don't spend the money. During the time that you did the exercise, you should have seen some results. The money you saved in the Treasure Chest should be given to charity or used to open a savings account in a bank.

Two people can use the same «Treasure Chest.»

Transcendental Method to Seal the Bathroom

You need approximately 9 grams of cinnabar, a small bottle of 150 proof liquor that is new, a bowl to mix the ingredients in and an eye dropper.

Use the following steps:

1. Take a deep breath and then say Heart Mantra while doing the Peace Mudra:

> Cate-Cate,
> Poro-Cate,
> Poro-Som-Cate,
> Bode-Soha

To do the Peace Mudra, place your right hand palm up near your solar plexus. Rest your left hand, palm up on top of the right. Join

130

the thumbs, letting them touch gently. Hold the hands in this position of reverence in front of your solar plexus.

After reciting the Heart Mantra nine times, continue with these steps:

2. Add the cinnabar to the bowl and with the eye dropper, add the number of drops equal to your age plus one, or add the number of drops equal to your age plus the ages of all the family members that live in the house, plus one additional drop, or add 99 or 108 drops.

3. Mix it together, men with the middle finger of the right hand and women with the middle finger of the left hand. As you are mixing, say the Six True Words Mantra: Om Man Ni Pad Me Hum.

4. Then go to the bathroom that you wish to seal and pour the mixture into the toilet. As you are doing this, reinforce your intention with the Three Secrets. Singing the Six True Words, visualize that you are sealing all possible drainage of positive Chi. Visualize that the infinite light projected through the spiritual Masters of humanity manifests an energy of peace, harmony and prosperity in the house or business. Visualize physical and spiritual abundance of the divine light infusing the space. When you are finished, visualize that your intentions are sealing all possibility that the water that goes down the drain will have a negative affect.

5. Fill the bowl with water and pour it into each drain in the house, including other bathrooms, sinks, floor or patio drains. As you are pouring out the contents of the bowl, sing the Six True Words Mantra. Try to estimate the amount to pour in each drain so that there is an equal portion for all the drains that you are sealing.

Wash your hands. After completing this method, be careful with the cinnabar powder. If there is any left over, keep it out of the reach of children and animals.

Activating Spiritual Power with the
Eight Trigrams Meditation

Use the Heart Mudra, recite the Peace Mantra nine times and visualize that everything around you dissolves into nothing.

Mantra:

Cate-Cate, Poro-Cate, Poro-Som-Cate, Bode-Soha.

The side of the Ba-Gua corresponding to the trigram «Chen»

1. Visualize yourself at the front door of your house or bedroom, and that your being is infused with light. Visualize that there is a small white ball of light at your «dan tien» (7 cm below your belly button). The sphere begins to change colors from white to gold and begins moving upward until it reaches the height of your eyes, where the golden sphere divides into three smaller ones with two of them in front of your eyes and one by your third eye. Visualize the three spheres projecting golden rays toward the wall that corresponds to the «Chen» trigram. Visualize the three rays engraving «Chen» or the symbol of the trigram on the wall in golden characters.

2. Visualize an immortal being dressed in a green, Chinese tunic with the symbol of the trigram «Chen» in gold on the center of his chest. The immortal approaches you blessing you and your family with health and good fortune.

3. The immortal returns to the «Chen» wall and disappears.

The corner of the Ba-Gua corresponding to the trigram «Sun»

1. Follow the same steps mentioned above. Visualize three golden rays emanating from the spheres toward the corner that corresponds to the trigram «Sun.» Visualize the three rays engraving «Sun» or the symbol of the trigram on the corner with the characters or lines in gold.

2. Visualize an immortal being dressed in a purple, Chinese tunic with the trigram «Sun» in gold on the center of his chest. The immortal approaches you and gives your precious gifts, money and treasures. He blesses you and your family so that your economic situation will be strengthened both at home and in your business.
3. The immortal returns to the «Sun» wall and disappears.

The side of the Ba-Gua corresponding to the trigram «Li»

1. Follow the same steps mentioned above. Visualize three golden rays emanating from the spheres toward the side that corresponds to the trigram «Li.» Visualize the three rays engraving «Li» or the trigram in golden characters on the wall.
2. Visualize an immortal being dressed in a red, Chinese tunic with the trigram «Li» in gold on the center of his chest. The immortal approaches you and blesses your path of progress so that your dreams become reality and that your fame and reputation are strengthened. Visualize your reputation expanding.
3. The immortal returns to the «Li» wall and disappears.

The corner corresponding to the trigram «Kun»

1. Visualize the three golden rays emanating from the spheres toward the corner that corresponds to the trigram «Kun.» «Kun» or the trigram is engraved on the corner in golden characters.
2. Visualize an immortal being dressed in a pink, Chinese tunic with the symbol of the trigram «Kun» in gold on the center of his chest. The immortal approaches you and blesses your mother and sisters. He also blesses the energy of associations, relationships and marriage. Whatever difficulty or disharmony that exists in this area is eliminated by the divine light of the immortal, so that all problems and difficulties are resolved and a happier life is manifested. Visualize all your problems and difficulties disappearing. If you are single and wish to marry, visualize marriage with your ideal partner.
3. The immortal returns to the «Kun» wall and disappears.

The side corresponding to the trigram «Tui»

1. Visualize an immortal being dressed in a white tunic with the trigram «Tui» in gold on his chest, or the symbol of «Tui» on the wall. The immortal activates your children's «third eye,» asking for their safety, health and/or a successful career or profession.
2. The immortal returns to the «Tui» wall and disappears.

The corner corresponding to the trigram «Ch'ien»

1. Visualize three golden rays emanating from the spheres toward the corner that corresponds to the trigram «Ch'ien,» and engraving «Ch'ien» or the trigram on it in golden characters.
2. Visualize an immortal being dressed in a gray tunic with the «Ch'ien» insignia in golden characters. The immortal comes with blessings to resolve any problems you have with your husband, father, or brothers.
3. After offering his blessing, the immortal returns to the corner where he came from and disappears.

The side corresponding to the trigram «Kan» of the Ba-Gua

1. Visualize three golden rays forming the letters or the trigram «Kan» in the corresponding wall of the Ba-Gua, as always in gold.
2. Visualize an immortal being emerging from the wall. He is dressed in a black tunic with the insignia «Kan» in brilliant gold on his chest. He approaches majestically performing the Blessing Mudra to bring protection from all difficulty and obstruction in the careers and professions of all those who live there.
3. The immortal returns to the «Kan» wall and disappears.

The corner corresponding to the trigram «Ken»

1. Visualize three golden rays emanating from the spheres toward the corner of the trigram «Ken,» engraving «Ken» or the trigram on the corner with the characters or lines in golden characters.
2. Visualize an immortal being dressed in a blue tunic with the «Ken» insignia in golden characters. The immortal approaches and transmits

his spiritual force, opening of your third eye to bring mental clarity, increase your capacity for knowledge, and help you cultivate the highest ideals of humanity.
3. The immortal returns to the «Ken» corner and disappears.

The Tai Chi

Visualize the «Tai Chi» or «Yin-Yang» symbol appearing in the center of the room. This is the center of all the trigrams of the Ba-Gua and of the creative universal force, Chi. Now visualize yourself in the center of the room. Keep your mind silent for a moment. Visualize the eight trigrams around the center and each immortal appearing from their respective positions. They now unite in a meditation asking for illumination in everyone's life and that they reached a better understanding of the laws of God. Visualize rays of light emanating from each immortal, in their respective color, illuminating and opening your mind to better understanding, tolerance and compassion. Feel the heat of the sphere of infinite light that encircles you, radiating from the center of your being, from the eternal flame of love that resides in your heart. Now, meditate on the transcendence of the moment. Visualize a sphere of transparent, brilliant, infinite light opening like a flower from the center of your heart and radiating toward the infinite. This light reaches toward your family, friends, house, office and the entire Universe. In your heart, ask God to grant a wish. Repeat the Six True Words. Visualize the light transforming into blessings. The immortals disappear slowly to their respective positions.

Master Lin Yun's Method of the I Ching Coins

Materials:

 A copy of the book, I Ching
 Six coins, one that is different from the rest

Steps:

1. Begin with the Three Secrets, the Peace Mudra and the Heart Mantra. Recite the Heart Mantra 9 or 27 times to relax your mind and heart. Visualize a pure light enveloping you.
2. Look to the sky and let your sight get lost in the distance.
3. Take a deep breath inhaling slowly through your nose in nine increments. Feel God with you in your heart. Watch for any impressions or images that may appear in your mind's eye.
4. Try to feel the images, feelings and experiences related to the question you wish to ask. In a sincere manner, ask for help, guidance and inspiration to find a solution or alternative. Write your question on a piece a paper and make a mental note of it.
5. Take the six coins in the palm of your hand and shake them nine times.
6. Stack them in your palm and then place them, one by one, on the table beginning with the coin on the bottom of the stack. Line them up vertically to create a hexagram. Make a note of where the «different» coin is positioned.
7. Figure out the hexagram by reading the Yin or Yang value of each coin (Before beginning, choose which side is Yin, which is Yang.) If you are using Chinese coins, the face with four symbols is Yang, the face with two is Yin.
8. Read the corresponding commentary and the line from the I Ching.
9. If you wish for further guidance or advice about your actions, use the position of the coin that is different to create another hexagram and read the corresponding commentary.

Strengthening your Personal Chi

This transcendental method removes negative influences and bad luck while strengthening the creative force.

You will need a small envelope of cinnabar, a small amount of 150 proof liquor and an eye dropper.

1. Men should place the cinnabar into the palm of their left hand while performing the Expelling Mudra. Women should use their right hand to hold the powder and do the mudra.
2. Use the eye dropper to add the number of drops equal to your age plus one on to the cinnabar in your hand. With each drop, say the mantra, Om Ma Ni Pad Me Hum.
3. Wet the middle finger of your free hand with the mixture and mark your left foot saying «OM,» visualizing the infinite and pure white light of Chi flowing from your left foot up through your body, opening a channel to your imagination and creativity.
4. Wet the middle finger of your free hand and mark your right foot while saying «MA,» visualize now that the Chi is red and flowing up your body infusing it with the power of divine will.
5. Wet the same finger again and mark your left hand saying «NI,» while visualizing yellow Chi inundating your body with light, strengthening its rhythms and harmonizing your mental and physical health.
6. Wet your finger again and mark the right hand saying «PAD,» visualizing green and feeling the vitalizing power of Chi that comes through time to connect you with the past and future and expand your consciousness, preparing you for new knowledge.
7. Wet your finger and bring it to the center of your chest, to the heart area. While saying «ME,» visualize blue Chi energy radiating from the depths of your being, inundating it with knowledge that comes from the spirit, the divine essence that resides in your heart.
8. End the exercise by bringing the middle finger of your free hand to your forehead saying «HUM.» Visualize the color black which represents the depths of your being. See how this energy, radiating through your forehead, opens a door that takes you into your internal Universe.

Note: Wash your hands carefully after this exercise.

Transcendental Method for Surgical Operations

Plants can be used as a transcendental method to insure a successful operation and rapid recovery. After asking permission from the patient, place nine small plants in a line between the bed and the door of the room where they are staying. Reinforce with the Three Secrets visualizing a successful operation, without complications, and a rapid recovery. The nine small plants can then be placed in a window so that no one trips over them.

Transcendental Method for Health

This transcendental method is known as «Yu-Nei» and is an important Tibetan Tantric Buddhist cure.
Connect each corner of the room with the middle of the opposite wall. Connect each corner with the opposing corner. The lines create a polygon in the central area (see the drawing on page 119). Place a live plant or a wind chime in that central area. Reinforce with the Three Secrets.

Transcendental Method for Back Pain

Place nine pieces of chalk in a dish that has a little uncooked rice in it. Place the dish under your bed, directly in line with the area of your back that hurts. Reinforce with the Three Secrets.

Transcendental Method for Heart Problems

This transcendental method can be used for heart disease or any type of medical treatment.
Place nine ice cubes on a white plate. Add a spoonful of camphor crystals. Reinforce with the Three Secrets. Place it under your bed aligned with your heart. Reinforce with the Three Secrets.

The Four Strings Transcendental Method

This transcendental method is used when you have problems that seem impossible to solve.

In each corner of the room, hang a red string from the ceiling to the floor. The strings symbolize the four legendary columns that supported the weight of the world. These strings also symbolize a kind of channel or line of communication that unites the universal consciousness, the source of all knowledge and wisdom, with Earth, invoking the powers of the Universe to illuminate your mind and intercede to eliminate your problems. Tie a small, 25 cm string in the center of each longer string. These short strings represent human beings. Reinforce this exercise with the Three Secrets.

Transcendental Method for Legal Difficulties

To resolve legal problems and avoid lawsuits, mix nine ice cubes with a spoonful of camphor crystals in a bowl (do this during your beneficial hours, according to Chinese astrology). Clean your stove top with this mixture for 15 minutes. Reinforce with the Three Secrets. Repeat daily for nine days.

Whenever you share this transcendental information with someone, you should honor the tradition of the red envelope.

佛

風水一生活的和諧 建角手冊

有緣讀者祈福增慧保健

寺禪林石揚兄硯

IV

PHILOSOPHIES RELATED TO FENG SHUI

陰陽

念慈書室主人林市隆題

九九二

Feng Shui students should be familiar with the following theories and philosophies:

1. Yin and Yang
2. The Tao
3. Chi
4. The I Ching and the Trigrams
5. The Theory of the Five Elements
6. The Theory of the Three Schools of Color
7. The Ba-Gua (The lines and symbols of harmony)
8. The Methods of the Tradition
9. The Transcendental Methods

Yin and Yang

Everything that is manifest in the Universe is accompanied by the principle of polarity. All energy and material forms have positive and negative polarities. Electrical energy consists of negative and positive charges. The atom is made up of a positively charged nucleus and negatively charged electrons. These apparently opposing polarities are in fact complimentary. The living cell is another example. It consists of a nucleus that guards and maintains the memory of its structure and system (Yang) and is surrounded by a covering that protects and receives light from its center (Yin). The solar system expresses the same principle on a much larger scale. The Sun radiates light (Yang) while the planets (Yin) receive its energy and warmth.

Yin is dark. Yang is luminous. Yin is feminine. Yang is masculine. Yin is empty. Yang is full. The Earth is Yin. The Sun is Yang. The mountains and valleys (with their passive attributes) are Yin; rivers and lakes (with their moving attributes) are Yang. Humans (Yang) live in the mountains and valleys and build their houses (Yin) where men (Yang) and women (Yin) live. Yin and Yang create the unity of Tao.

Yang emanates from the external Universe and its light, positive and divine polarity radiates from the infinite, from the galaxies, stars and Sun.

Yin emanates from the interior Universe and its essence of negative and spiritual polarity radiates from the infinitesimal, from the rhythmic center of life, from the seeds, the planets and Earth.

Yin and Yang correspond to the four season of the year. Spring corresponds to the east and Yang and Yin; summer is south and Yang; fall is west and Yin and Yang; winter is north and Yin.

SOME ATTRIBUTES OF YIN AND YANG	
YIN	YANG
ZERO	ONE
NOTHING	ALL
MOON	SUN
CURVE	ANGULAR
NEGATIVE	POSITIVE
PASSIVE	ACTIVE
BLACK	WHITE
INFINITESIMAL	INFINITE
EARTH	HEAVEN
LOW	HIGH
SOFT	HARD
SUBJECTIVE	OBJECTIVE
UNCONSCIOUS	CONSCIOUS
SPIRITUAL	MATERIAL
ELECTRON	PROTON
WATER	WIND
HOUSE	FAMILY
WOMAN	MAN
MOTHER	FATHER
NORTH	SOUTH
MOUNTAIN	WATER

The Tao

The origin of this philosophy is lost in the beginnings of Chinese civilization and is based on their intimate relationship with nature. The Tao is the source of all existence. It is the unity that is never visible and the source from which everything flows in expanding vibrations, manifesting the world and nature. The opposing yet complementary aspects of Yin and Yang create the unity of Tao.

Nature's shapes, substances, colors and cycles reveal the principles of its manifestation and its relation to man as an integral element in the evolution of life on our planet.

Earth is a reflection of the Universe. Its eternal and harmonious laws are projected into the different levels of existence according to universal principles.

One of those universal principles is Duality or Polarity.

The logical = «ru-shr» = is the external, Yang

The illogical = «chu-shr» = the transcendental, Yin

The Universal Creative Force - Chi

Chi is the creative force of the Universe, the essence of the manifestation of life. It circulates from the center of Earth and is projected from the Sun, the center of our solar system, as well as from the Universe. It is the force that creates mountains, directs rivers, maintains the oceans and the rhythm of all that exists in nature. It is the source and guide for the evolution of the mineral, plant, animal and human realms. Not only is man a channel for this force that circulates through him, he is also conscious of its existence.

Chi flows throughout nature. It moves through the acupuncture meridians of the human body. In the countryside, it manifests through fertile harvests, fruit, plants, forest and prairies. In the atmosphere and oceans, it governs the climatic and energetic changes that we experience as atmospheric and maritime currents. Among the various forms of Chi we can mention «Sheng Chi» and «Ssu Chi.» Sheng Chi is active, positive and energetic. Its force and potency is manifested each day as Yang, during the hours the sun is rising -from midnight to midday. Ssu Chi is passive, negative and regenerating. Its effect is manifested each day as Yin, as the sun is setting -from midday to midnight.

Chi is also known by other names such as, prana, nous, breath of life (ruach), vital life force, etc... There are infinite levels of Chi both on Earth as well as in the Universe.

The Trigrams

The trigrams are symbolic expressions of the basic combinations of Yin and Yang. They are combinations of two values, in units of three. They are manifestations of the universal principle of duality, expressed through the positive and negative values of Yin and Yang, in third dimensional space.

The maximum number of combinations, of two values in groups of three, is equal to the number 2 to the third power (2 x 2 x 2) or 8.

The Chinese tradition describes how the great philosopher, Fu Hsi, came up with the trigrams. As he was meditating on the shore of a lake, around 3,000 AC, he observed the shell of a tortoise that was slowly emerging from the water. Fu Hsi saw that the shell's surface had two types of lines, some broken, others solid. The vision of these symbols illuminated his mind and gave him answers to questions he and other truth seekers had been searching for. These questions were related to the principle of duality, how day moved into night, the existence of men and women, and Yang and Yin. Fu Hsi assigned the value of Yang to the solid line and Yin to the broken line.

The development of the theory of Yin and Yang in three dimensions is summarized by the total number of combinations of the 8 symbols. These symbols have different manifestations and correspondences in nature such as the cardinal directions, the Chinese elements, the colors, the planets and life activities of human beings.

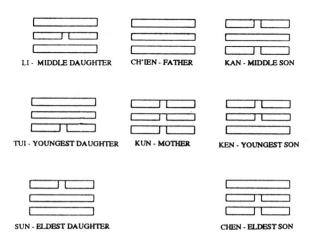

LI - MIDDLE DAUGHTER   CH'IEN - FATHER   KAN - MIDDLE SON

TUI - YOUNGEST DAUGHTER   KUN - MOTHER   KEN - YOUNGEST SON

SUN - ELDEST DAUGHTER   CHEN - ELDEST SON

Family relationship of the Eight Trigrams

The Creation of the First Heaven Ba-Gua

Fu Hsi elaborated on the symbolism of the trigrams and used them to create an octagon known as the Ba-Gua of the First Heaven or the «Ba-Gua of Fu Hsi.» Ba-Gua means «eight lines or symbols.»

In the Ba-Gua, the trigrams are arranged as if the observer where positioned in the center of the octagon.

The lines of harmony of the Ba-Gua originate in the universal principle of duality, Yin and Yang. Yin and Yang in combination are manifested in the trigrams and hexagrams. The trigrams used in the Ba-Gua evolved in the following way:

The universal principle of duality:

Yang   Yin

The binary combinations were born and manifested the Four Primary Pairs.

Yang Yang	Yin Yin
Yang Yin	Yin Yang

From the Four Primary Pairs, the Eight Trigrams were born. The trigrams combined the two primary values of Yin and Yang in groups of three within the three dimensions of our physical Universe.

Chen	Li	Kun	Ken	Tui	Ch'ien	Kan	Sun

Fu Hsi positioned these symbols on the First Heaven Ba-Gua, as follows:

☰	☴	☵	☶	☷	☳	☲	☱
Ch'ien Father S Yang	Sun Daughter 1 SW Yin	Kan Daughter 2 W Yang	Ken Son 3 NW Yang	Kun Mother N Yin	Chen Son 1 NE Yang	Li Daughter 2 E Yin	Tui Daughter 3 SE Yin

The First Heaven Ba-Gua represent the Universe before the manifestations of forms in the present world.

The Fu Hsi Ba-Gua is the one usually found in Chinese establishments and stores. The power of this Ba-Gua lies in the harmony of its symbols. If we count the number of lines, we find that the sum of the two opposing symbols is always 9. The number 9 is sacred in Chinese philosophy. It represents the perfect combination, in this case the sum of the eight sides of the Ba-Gua plus its center.

Hanging the Fu Hsi Ba-Gua over the front door (on the outside), helps to balance and harmonize the energies of a home or work place. It also protects against negative thoughts or situations. The Ba-Gua is hung with the trigram «Ch'ien,» or father (3 lines), at the top; the trigram «Kun,» or mother (6 lines), is then at the bottom. If the back door also need protection, hang two Ba-Guas, one on the outside, with «Ch'ien» at the top as described before, and one on the inside of the same wall at approximately the same height. The Ba-Gua on the inside should have the «Kun» trigram on the top, and «Ch'ien» on the bottom. The father -Ch'ien- protects and harmonizes energies that come from the outside; and the mother -Kun- nurtures and harmoniously transforms energy inside the house.

148

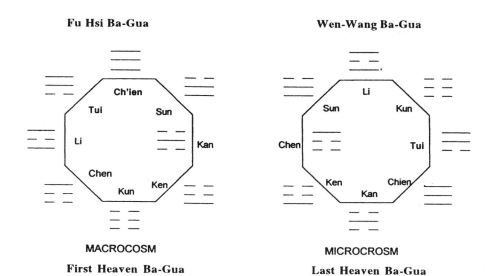

Fu Hsi Ba-Gua

MACROCOSM

First Heaven Ba-Gua

Wen-Wang Ba-Gua

MICROCROSM

Last Heaven Ba-Gua

The Creation of the Last Heaven Ba-Gua

Many years later, another Chinese philosopher, Wen Wang (the founder of the Chou Dynasty, 1231-1135 AC) changed the position of the symbols on the octagon to reflect the creative force in harmony with nature. This Ba-Gua is known as the last heaven Ba-Gua.

The trigrams are arranged as follows:

Li 1Daughter 2 S Fire Red Yin	Kun Mother SW Earth Pink Yin	Tui Daughter 3 W Metal White Yin	Ch'ien Father NW Metal Gray Yang	Kan Son 2 N Water Black Yang	Ken Son 3 NE Earth Blue Yang	Chen Son 1 E Wood Green Yang	Sun Daughter 1 SE Wood Purple Yin

In the Black Hat School, the last heaven Ba-Gua is used for transcendental methods in the same way as the Fu Hsi Ba-Gua.

The Correspondences of the Trigrams of the Last Heaven Ba-Gua

According to the last heaven or Wen Wang Ba-Gua, the trigrams have the following symbolism:

LI
Represents fame, the color red, the fire element, the south, and other correspondences such as: the Phoenix, the Sun, lightning, and the human eye.
Hours: from 12 - 3 p.m.

KUN
Represents marriage, pink (red and white), southeast and other correspondences such as: mother, nature, figures, compassion, clothes and the solar plexus.
Hours: from 3 - 6 p.m.

TUI
Represents children, white, metal, west and other correspondences such as: the youngest daughter, steam, clouds, placid lakes, spirit and the mouth.
Hours: from 6 - 9 p.m.

CH'IEN
Represents benefactors, gray (white and black), northeast and other correspondences such as: father, firmament, Universe and the head.
Hours: from 9 p.m. 12 a.m.

KAN
Represents profession, black, water, north and other correspondences such as: evolved spirits, hidden things, warriors, tortoise, crab, rivers, the depth of the ocean, the abysm and the ears.
Hours: from 12 - 3 a.m.

KEN
Represents knowledge, blue, southeast and other correspondences such as: mountains, rocks, personal enrichment and the hands.
Hours: from 3 - 6 a.m.

150

CHEN   Represents family, green, wood, east and other correspondences such as: lightning, the eldest son, high roads, evolution and the feet.
Hours: from 6 - 9 a.m.

SUN-   Represents finances, purple, northeast, and other correspondences such as: wind, heights, the eldest daughter and hips.
Hours: from 9 a.m. - 12 p.m.

To determine the Yin or Yang polarity of a trigram, simply count the number of lines, including any of the broken lines. If the total is even, it is a Yin trigram. If the total is odd, it is Yang.

Examples:

The trigram «Ch'ien,» benefactors, has 3 lines, an uneven number, so it is Yang.
The trigram "Kan," career and profession has 5 lines, an uneven number, so it is Yang.

The I Ching

The I Ching is a system of philosophy that studies the process of change in human existence and the Universe. The I Ching uses the system of the trigrams to represent life's activities. Yin is symbolized by a broken line, Yang by a solid line.

Two trigrams make up a hexagrams - 2 values, Yin and Yang, in groups of six. The total number of hexagrams in the I Ching is equal to 2 to the sixth power (2 x 2 x 2 x 2 x 2 x 2) or 64 symbols.

Students of Feng Shui do not have to study the theories of the I Ching in depth; they should simply be familiar with the trigrams.

The Five Chinese Elements

Creative energy or Chi flows through all that is manifest and can be adjusted to benefit those who create the space. Material forms manifested by creative energy were categorized by the ancient Chinese as the following five elements:

1. Wood
2. Fire
3. Earth
4. Metal
5. Water

Each of the five Chinese elements corresponds to a color, a direction, a human activity or life area, among other things. The elements are also related to Chinese astrology and the I Ching.

Those who use Feng Shui are creating spatial environments. This art helps expand consciousness and establish subtle communication with the elements of the space. Within a space we can hear the silent echo of the emanations of our history, memories and our very lives. As we become one with the true nature of our homes, we use our intuition to rearrange objects, add color and change shapes.

When we move objects, we begin playing with spatial elements and reinforce certain aspects of our lives. When the elements and colors in our home are balanced, the spirit of the space is harmonized, and our lives begin to change.

The most important aspect of the Theory of the Five Chinese Elements is understanding the Constructive and Destructive Cycles of the Elements.

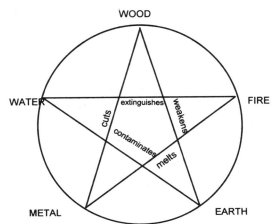

The Cycle of the Five Elements

The Constructive Cycle of the Five Chinese Elements

The order or sequence of the five Chinese elements determines the degree of harmony present in a space. The Constructive Cycle of the Five Elements is based on observations from nature. This is the generative sequence:

1. Wood   feeds
2. Fire   which creates ashes to produce
3. Earth   which over time creates
4. Metal   which when cooling creates
5. Water   which feeds...wood

and this is how one element in the cycle generates the next.

The Destructive Cycle of the Five Chinese Elements

In skipping the natural sequence of the five elements as described above, imbalance or disharmony is created:

1. Wood   Skipping fire, takes nutrients from
2. Earth   Skipping metal, contaminates
3. Water   Skipping wood, puts out
4. Fire   Skipping earth, melts
5. Metal   Skipping water, cuts...wood.

When an element skips its natural sequence, it destroys the next element.

Wood is fed by water which destroys fire.
Fire is fed by wood which destroys earth.
Earth is born of fire which destroys metal.
Metal is born of the earth which contaminates water.
Water is born of metal which destroys wood.

According to Fu Hsi, the five elements express the subtle essence of Chi, though its true nature is merely approximated by these five objects. The elements represent the creative force of nature and the Universe. The five

153

colors, five senses, five fingers, five major organs and five magic planets, among others are derived from the workings of this force.

The Reductive Cycle of the Elements

This cycle is the inverse of the constructive cycle.

Fire burns wood.
Wood absorbs water.
Water corrodes or weakens metal.
Metal exhausts earth.
Earth puts out fire.

Observing and understanding these qualities is important when harmonizing a space, as they help reduce the force of an aggressive element.

The Relationship between the Elements

When we relate and apply the three sequences: constructive, destructive and reductive cycles, we find some very interesting relationships that can help in creating a space.

The elements are related to one another. Water over metal produces an ideal relationship because metal manifests water. Water over wood, or their corresponding colors black over green has a weakening effect. Wood over water, green over black, has a positive effect.

RELATIONSHIP AMONG THE ELEMENTS					
HABITAT	AMBIENTAL ELEMENT (BELOW)				
(ABOVE)	WOOD	FIRE	EARTH	METAL	WATER
WOOD	Stable	Weak	Control	Conflict	Ideal
FIRE	Ideal	Stable	Weak	Control	Conflict
EARTH	Conflict	Ideal	Stable	Weak	Control
METAL	Control	Conflict	Ideal	Stable	Weak
WATER	Weak	Control	Conflict	Ideal	Stable

Each of the five Chinese elements corresponds to a variety of manifestations including shapes, colors and personality types:

WOOD   Wood corresponds to furniture and accessories made of wood; plants, flowers, trees, artificial or dried plants and flowers; paintings and photos with trees; green areas; all types of fabric; wall paper; cylindrical shapes, columns, posts; greens and blues, among others.

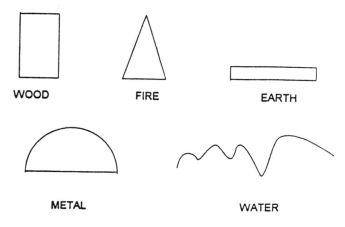

The Shapes of the Five Elements

FIRE   Fire corresponds to pets; products derived from animals such as feathers, bones, leather or wool; pictures and photos of people and animals; conical or pyramid shapes; and the color red, among others.

EARTH Earth corresponds to objects made of plaster, mud, ceramic, tiles, bricks; works of art and photos of the desert, mountains or valleys; square and rectangular shapes; flat and horizontal surfaces; and the colors ochre and yellow, among others.

METAL Metal corresponds to mineral rocks and any type of metal including iron, copper, bronze, silver and gold; works of art made from metal; oval shapes and arches; and the color white, among others.

WATER   Water corresponds to lakes, rivers, the sea; water fountains and water falls; mirrors and glass; art pieces related to the sea and pictures and photos with water motifs; asymmetrical and undulating shapes; the colors gray, dark blue and black.

The following are the correspondences of the major organs of the body and the elements:

ORGAN	ELEMENT	COLOR
Heart	Fire	Red
Stomach	Earth	Yellow
Lungs	Metal	White
Liver	Wood	Green
Kidneys	Water	Black

The Theory of the Three Schools of Colors

In Feng Shui, as taught by Master Lin Yun and the Black Hat School, the harmonious use of colors follows the theories of the Three Schools of Colors:

1. The Theory of the Colors of the Five Elements
2. The Theory of the Colors of the Rainbow
3. The Theory of the Colors of the Six True Words

The Theory of the Colors of the Five Chinese Elements deals with the use of color within a space in its external or Yang aspect.

The Theory of the Colors of the Rainbow involves using the colors of the psychic body. It is the use of color in its internal or Yin aspect.

The Theory of the Colors of the Six True Words reveals the effect that color has on the spirit. This is the use of color in its integral or Tao aspect.

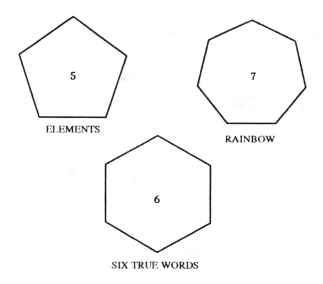

ELEMENTS

RAINBOW

SIX TRUE WORDS

The Three Schools of Colors

1. The Colors and the Five Elements

The philosophy of the Five Elements is based on using the elements in a harmonious, constructive and vitalizing way to channel Chi with more strength and harmony. According to the principles of Feng Shui taught by Tantric Buddhism, the elements should be chosen for their beauty, natural harmony and creative force. If these principles are not used or understood, the space could reflect weak and stagnant Chi that could in turn manifest in negative or inharmonious ways.

Each of the Five Elements: water, wood, fire, earth and metal can be represented with a color. The elements manifest harmoniously in nature, one emanating from another in circles or spirals of vibrant light. From water, wood is born; wood manifest and feeds fire; fire transmutes the elements into ash to manifest earth; from earth, metal is born; metal gives birth to water; water nurtures wood, and so on.

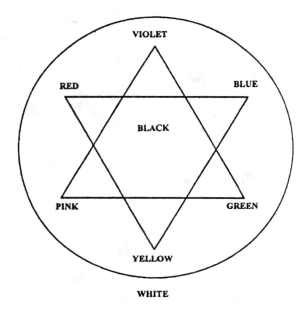

The Star of Colors

In the Destructive Cycle of the Five Elements: wood erodes earth; earth contaminates water; water extinguishes fire; fire melts metal; and metal cuts wood.

The colors associated with the five elements are: water (black), wood (green), fire (red), earth (yellow, orange) and metal (white). Each element is associated with an activity in our lives. Each of these activities is honored in a circle or area within our homes and work places.

Using colors is very important in Feng Shui. The philosophy of colors and their application has been described in depth in the book, Living Color, by Master Thomas Lin Yin and Sarah Rossbach. By honoring the presence of color in Feng Shui decoration, we balance and harmonize the force of Chi that manifests through the five elements.

ELEMENT	COLOR	DIRECTION	QUALITIES
WOOD	GREEN	EAST	VITALITY, INITIATION, BENEVOLENCE
FIRE	RED	SOUTH	WILL, REALIZATION, COURTESY
EARTH	YELLOW	CENTER	BALANCE, INTUITION, COMPASSION
METAL	WHITE	WEST	IMAGINATION, CREATIVITY, PURITY
WATER	BLACK	NORTH	MEDITATION, JUSTICE, POTENTIAL

Each of these qualities or activities also corresponds to an area in the home or work place based on the Ba-Gua. Using the constructive cycle of the elements, we can create a harmonious space. Using colors in their corresponding areas reinforces the life activity related to that area.

An example of how we use colors happens every morning. As we dress, we decide what type of clothes and colors we are going to wear based on what we have planned for the day. Often we choose a color based on subjective reasons influenced by the following:

1. What is happening that day.
2. Subjective attraction.
3. Situation or availability.
4. transcendent decision.

You can decorate a room or a whole house with the colors that correspond to the lines of harmony or life areas of the Ba-Gua.

ACTIVITY	ELEMENT	COLORS
FINANCES	WOOD/FIRE	GREEN, PURPLE AND RED
FAME	FIRE	RED
MARRIAGE	FIRE/METAL	RED, PINK AND WHITE
CHILDREN	METAL	PASTELS AND WHITE
BENEFACTORS	METAL/WATER	WHITE, GRAY AND BLACK
PROFESSION	WATER	DARK BLUE AND BLACK
KNOWLEDGE	WATER/WOOD	BLACK, BLUE AND GREEN
HEALTH	EARTH	YELLOW AND EARTH COLOR

2. The Seven Colors of the Rainbow School

The Seven Colors of the Rainbow School is based on our body's energetic centers. The mystical schools in the west have established the following correspondences between the psychic centers and colors:

CENTER	COLOR
PINEAL GLAND	PURPLE
PITUITARY GLAND	INDIGO
THROAT	BLUE
CHEST	GREEN
SOLAR PLEXUS	YELLOW
ADRENAL GLANDS	ORANGE
SACRUM	RED

The transcendental method of Feng Shui includes Buddhist and Tibetan meditations for elevating and transmuting Chi through the energy centers of the body or the chakras. However, these can be substituted for the others in keeping with your religious traditions. What is important is establishing an intimate connection with the divinity, not what name is used or what words or prayers are said.

3. The Colors of the Six True Words Mantra

The sacred mantra of the Six True Words is related to color as follows:

Om	–	White - Feet to knees
Ma	–	Red - Knees to hips
Ni	–	Yellow - Hips to solar plexus
Pad	–	Green - Solar plexus to throat
Me	–	Blue - Throat to third eye
Hum	–	Black - Third eye to crown of the head

When used properly, the colors of the Six True Words Mantra: Om Man Ni Pad Me Hum, will illuminate the mind and heart with the resplendent light of the divine presence.

The colors derived from the vibratory power of the Six True Words Mantra radiate from the chakras and are reflected in the physical body. This method is wholly transcendental.

The following figure shows the natural scale of the colors and their relationship with each syllable of the mantra Om Ma Ni Pad Me Hum.

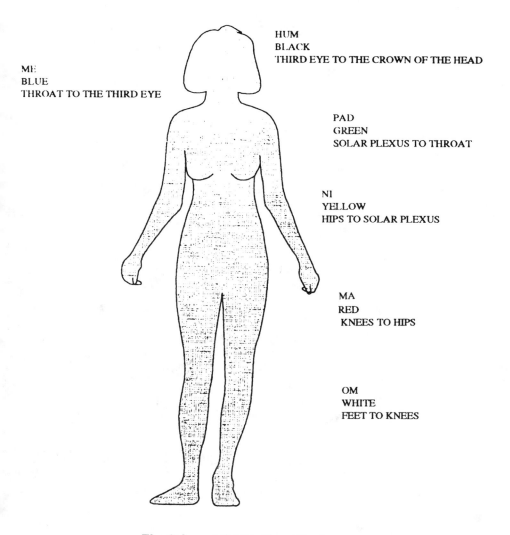

HUM
BLACK
THIRD EYE TO THE CROWN OF THE HEAD

ME
BLUE
THROAT TO THE THIRD EYE

PAD
GREEN
SOLAR PLEXUS TO THROAT

NI
YELLOW
HIPS TO SOLAR PLEXUS

MA
RED
KNEES TO HIPS

OM
WHITE
FEET TO KNEES

The Colors of the Six True Words

V

CHINESE ASTROLOGY

Just as with the I Ching, a Feng Shui student does not need to be an expert in Chinese astrology. It is only necessary to know the value of the trigrams of the I Ching and the favorable days and hours for Feng Shui.

Chinese astrology is based on the movements of the Moon. The Chinese Zodiac has twelve signs, each symbolized by an animal. Each sign corresponds to a year as well as a time of day. So, everyone has a favorable time of the day based on the year that they were born.

The following table shows the hours, elements and colors that correspond to each Chinese astrological sign:

Month	Symbol	Hour	Element	Color	Year
1	Ox (Bull, Bear)	1-3 am	Water	Black	1901
2	Tiger	3-5 am	Wood/East	Blue	1902
3	Hare (Rabbit, cat)	5-7 am	Wood/East	Green	1903
4	Dragon	7-9 am	Wood/East	Green	1904
5	Snake	9-11 am	Fire/South	Purple	1905
6	Horse	11-1 pm	Fire/South	Red	1906
7	Goat	1-3 pm	Fire/South	Red	1907
8	Monkey	3-5 pm	Metal/West	Pink	1908
9	Rooster	5-7 pm	Metal/West	White	1909
10	Dog	7-9 pm	Metal/West	White	1910
11	Boar	9-11 pm	Water/North	Gray	1911
12	Rat	11-1 am	Water	Black	1900

The year 1900 was the year of the Rat, sign number 12 (or 0).

Besides the favorable hours for each sign, there are also three additional times that are beneficial for each person based on the year they were born, these are:

1. The hour that correspond with the sign parallel to the birth sign. The parallel sign is the sign (number) that when added to the birth sign, gives a total of 13. For example, if the birth sign is Ox (number 1) then the parallel sign is Rat (number 12) as 1 and 12 add to 13.

2. The two hours that correspond to the signs that are trine to the birth sign. A trine is 120°. Each sign in Chinese astrology, just as in conventional astrology, occupies 30°. So, within each trine, there are four signs. To find which signs form a trine with the birth sign, add the numbers 4 and 8 to it. For example, if the birth sign is Ox (1) the compatible signs are Snake which is 5 (1+4=5) and Rooster which is 9 (1+8=9)

To determine which hours of the day are favorable, divide the last two digits of the birth year by 12. The remainder of this number is the number of the astrological sign in the table above.

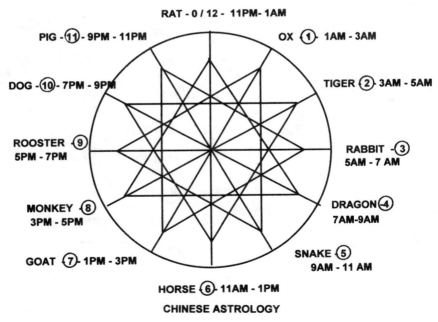

RAT - 0 / 12 - 11PM- 1AM

PIG -⑪- 9PM - 11PM   OX ① 1AM - 3AM

DOG -⑩- 7PM - 9PM   TIGER ② 3AM - 5AM

ROOSTER ⑨
5PM - 7PM   RABBIT -③
5AM - 7 AM

MONKEY ⑧
3PM - 5PM   DRAGON④
7AM-9AM

GOAT ⑦- 1PM - 3PM   SNAKE ⑤
9AM - 11 AM

HORSE ⑥ 11AM - 1PM

CHINESE ASTROLOGY

Example:

Birth Year = 1937

1. Divide the last two digits «37» by 12.
2. 37 ÷ 12 = 3 with a remainder of 1
3. The astrological sign corresponding to 1 is Ox.
4. The most favorable hours are 1 - 3 a.m.
5. The compatible signs and hours are

by trine: 5 (1+4) and 9 (1+8) so they are Snake (9 - 11 a.m.)
and Rooster (5 - 7 p.m.)

by parallel: 12 (13-1) is the Rat (11 p.m. - 1 a.m.)

So the best hours are: 1 - 3 a.m. by birth
9 - 11 a.m. by trine
5 - 7 p.m. by trine
11 p.m. - 1 a.m. by parallel

We can also combine the best hours of the day with the most favorable days of the year. These days are calculated based on the position of the Moon. The best days are the New Moon and 14 days after the New Moon.

Description of the Chinese Astrological Signs

0 OR 12 RAT

(Years: 1900, 1912, 1924, 1936, 1948, 1960, 1972, 1984, 1996)
Those born during the year of the rat are friendly, funny, honest and meticulous. Generally, they are good advisors but cannot make decisions by themselves. They are sometimes greedy and the desire for power may lead them to gambling and dependency.
Hours: 11 p.m. - 1 a.m.

1 OX

(Years: 1901, 1913, 1925, 1937, 1949, 1961, 1973, 1985, 1997)
Strong, hard working and methodical, they enjoy helping others.
Colors: Black, green and dark green.
Hours: 1 - 3 a.m.

2 TIGER

(Years: 1902, 1914, 1926, 1938, 1950, 1962, 1974, 1986, 1998)
Energetic and charismatic, they are excellent leaders and protectors.
Generally, they do not like working for others. Color: Black, green
and dark green.
Hours: 3 - 5 a.m.

3 HARE

(Years: 1903, 1915, 1927, 1939, 1951, 1963, 1975, 1987, 1999)
They are very intelligent, agile and ambitious, but easily distracted.
They are calm and attentive. Color: Green or blue.
Hours: 5 - 7 a.m.

4 DRAGON

(Years: 1904, 1916, 1928, 1940, 1952, 1964, 1976, 1988, 2000)
Strong, robust, they are intuitive, artistic and lucky. They possess
spiritual abilities. Colors: Blue, green, pink and purple.
Hours: 7 - 9 a.m.

5 SNAKE

(Years: 1905, 1917, 1929, 1941, 1953, 1965, 1977, 1989, 2001)
They are also called «little dragon.» This is considered a year of good
luck. Snakes are knowledgeable, considerate and calm. In general
snakes are successful, but they can become envious and selfish
when confronted. Colors: Blue, green, pink and purple.
Hours: 9 - 11 a.m.

6 HORSE

(Years: 1906, 1918, 1930, 1942, 1954, 1966, 1978, 1990, 2002)
They have a pleasing and positive character. Diligent and agile, the
horse is strong and direct though sometimes rude. Colors: red and
pink.
Hours: 11 a.m. - 1 p.m.

7 GOAT

(Years: 1907, 1919, 1931, 1943, 1955, 1967, 1979, 1991, 2003)

Those born in the year of the goat are naturally artistic and business oriented. Well mannered and altruistic, they tend to have family problems. They are also inclined to be melancholy. Colors: crimson, red and pink.

Hours: 1 - 3 p.m.

8 MONKEY

(Years: 1908, 1920, 1932, 1944, 1956, 1968, 1980, 1992, 2004)

Monkeys are friendly and creative by nature. They like to solve problems. They are very intelligent and opportunistic. They can sometimes be slow in paying their debts. Colors: red and pink.

Hours: 3 - 5 p.m.

9 ROOSTER

(Years: 1909, 1921, 1933, 1945, 1957, 1969, 1981, 1993, 2005)

Resourceful, hard working and talented. They are sometimes arrogant and proud which alienates them from family and friends. Colors: White.

Hours 5 - 7 p.m.

10 DOG

(Years: 1910, 1922, 1934, 1946, 1958, 1970, 1982, 1994, 2006)

Honest, loyal with a great sense of justice. Dogs inspire trust and reach their goals quickly. They are tireless workers and always on the defensive. Colors: White, gray and black.

Hours: 7 - 9 p.m.

11 Boar

(Years: 1911, 1923, 1935, 1947, 1959, 1971, 1983, 1995, 2007)

Sensitive, generous and indulgent. Sometimes their indulgence leads to gluttony which is their weakness. Their generous nature allows people to take advantage of them. They don't know how to defend themselves. Indecisive and insecure. Fortunately they tend to be happy. Colors: White, gray and black.

Hours: 9 - 11 p.m.

CHINESE ASTROLOGY TABLE
CALCULATION OF PROPITIOUS TIMES AND COMPATIBLE SIGNS

RAT	OX	TIGER	RABBIT	DRAGON	SNAKE	HORSE	GOAT	MONKEY	ROOSTER	DOG	PIG
11pm-1am	1am-3am	3am-5am	5am-7am	7am-9am	9am-11am	11am-1pm	1pm-3pm	3pm-5pm	5pm-7pm	7pm-9pm	9pm-11pm
1900	1901	1902	1903	1904	1905	1906	1907	1908	1909	1910	1911
1912	1913	1914	1915	1916	1917	1918	1919	1920	1921	1922	1923
1924	1925	1926	1927	1928	1929	1930	1931	1932	1933	1934	1935
1936	1937	1938	1939	1940	1941	1942	1943	1944	1945	1946	1947
1948	1949	1950	1951	1952	1953	1954	1955	1956	1957	1958	1959
1960	1961	1962	1963	1964	1965	1966	1967	1968	1969	1970	1971
1972	1973	1974	1975	1976	1977	1978	1979	1980	1981	1982	1983
1984	1985	1986	1987	1988	1989	1990	1991	1992	1993	1994	1995
1996	1997	1998	1999	2000	2001	2002	2003	2004	2005	2006	2007
2008	2009	2010	2011	2012	2013	2014	2015	2016	2017	2018	2019
12 0 0	1	2	3	4	5	6	7	8	9	10	11

COMPATIBLE SIGNS

TRINE

RAT	OX	TIGER	RABBIT	DRAGON	SNAKE	HORSE	GOAT	MONKEY	ROOSTER	DOG	PIG
TRINE				TRINE				TRINE			
	TRINE				TRINE				TRINE		
		TRINE				TRINE				TRINE	
			TRINE				TRINE				TRINE

PARALLEL SIGNS

RAT	OX	TIGER	RABBIT	DRAGON	SNAKE	HORSE	GOAT	MONKEY	ROOSTER	DOG	PIG
PARALLEL	PARALLEL										
		PARALLEL									PARALLEL
			PARALLEL							PARALLEL	
				PARALLEL					PARALLEL		
					PARALLEL			PARALLEL			
						PARALLEL	PARALLEL				

CORRESPONDENCIAS:

	RAT	OX	TIGER	RABBIT	DRAGON	SNAKE	HORSE	GOAT	MONKEY	ROOSTER	DOG	PIG
	WATER	EARTH	EARTH	WOOD	WOOD	WOOD	FIRE	EARTH	EARTH	METAL	METAL	METAL
	BLACK	YELLOW	YELLOW	GREEN	GREEN	GREEN	RED	YELLOW	YELLOW	WHITE	WHITE	WHITE
	NORTH	CENTER	CENTER	EAST	EAST	EAST	SOUTH	CENTER	CENTER	WEST	WEST	WEST
	TURTLE	SNAKE	SNAKE	DRAGON	DRAGON	DRAGON	PHOENIX	SNAKE	SNAKE	TIGER	TIGER	TIGER
	KAN	KENKUN	KENKUN	CHENSUN	CHENSUN	CHENSUN	LI	KENKUN	KENKUN	CHIENTUI	CHIENTUI	CHIENTUI

VI

THE ELEMENTS
AND PERSONALITY

The entire Universe is in movement. The cells of our bodies are constantly changing, just as our thoughts and emotions do. Our personalities are manifested according to the environment we are in and our character. Personality is external in nature and reflects the moment we are experiencing. Character is internal in nature and reflects and contains the essence of the elements. Each person has characteristics of each element in varying quantities. Just being conscious of these elements within us, helps us to make better decisions in our lives. The amount of each element we have determines the balance between body and soul.

WOOD

People who have very little of the wood element are quiet, without opinions, and easily swayed. A person with the wood element in balance is strong natured, but open to other's opinions. Excessive wood makes a person inflexible and stubborn. They do not listen to others especially when they don't agree with them.

When there is an imbalance in the wood element, there are physical symptoms that manifest such as dizziness, abdominal and joint pain.

To adjust an imbalance of too much or too little wood, place three live plants, one just inside the front door, one just inside the door to the living room and the other inside the bedroom door. Visualize the wood element in balance and reinforce with the Three Secrets for 9 or 27 days.

FIRE

 When the fire element is low, a person is weak when it comes to making decisions and following through, and often they allow themselves to be stepped on. A person with balanced fire is fair, diplomatic and capable of resolving problems with their family, friendships and associates. They are very good managers. When a person has too much fire, they become restless, critical and volatile. To adjust fire imbalances (too much or too little) practice the heart meditation. If there is too much fire, practice the breathing exercise with the light of the Moon; and if there is too little, with sunlight.

When there is a fire imbalance, it can manifest as depression, circulation problems, heart problems and insomnia.

EARTH

When a person has too little of the earth element, they become opportunistic, envious and selfish. If the earth element is balanced, the person is sincere, generous and trustworthy. A person with too much of the earth element is too quick to give in, gives away everything they have and goes to extremes with self sacrifice. To adjust too much or too little earth element, place nine small, round stones in a clay or crystal jar with water. Pick your favorite color. Place the jar under your bed. Visualize the earth element. Reinforce with the Three Secrets. Change the water each day, tossing it outside the house. Do this for 9 or 27 days. For more emphasis, and to cultivate your profession or career, add a green leaf to the water.

An imbalance of the earth element can manifest physical symptoms such as ulcers, digestive problems and an excessive urge to eat sweets.

METAL

People with very little metal are timid, calm and cautious. They are very quiet and seldom show their emotions. If the metal element is in balance, the person is well spoken and is a good listener. An excess of metal makes a person talk too much and say things without thinking.

When the metal element is weak, yellow clothing should be worn. Yellow corresponds to the earth element. Earth creates metals. Another solution is to take a nonmetallic ring and place it under the mattress (between the mattress and the base of the bed) in the area that corresponds to children (metal), and sleep with it for nine days. Afterwards, wear the ring on your middle or pinkie finger, men on the left hand, women on the right. Reinforce with the Three Secrets. When there is an over abundance of metal, it is a good idea to use red which corresponds to fire. Fire melts metal. Another solution is to swallow saliva three times before speaking.

Some of physical symptoms associated with an imbalance of metal are bronchitis and dry skin.

WATER

The Chinese divide the water element into two categories, still water and moving water. Still water is seen as introspection or intuitive power. Those who lack  this aspect are unaware of their psychic capacities; Chi does not reach their consciousness. They are closed-minded and ignorant. This type of person doesn't worry about society or what is happening in the world. They are only concerned with their personal problems. Those who have the still water element in balance are like a deep and transparent lake that reflects the sunlight from its depths. These people are clear minded, intelligent, intuitive and dedicated to spiritual work. A person with a lot of this element has an expansive and dynamic intelligence focused on the practical and material. To adjust imbalances in this element, use the Sun and Moon mirror exercise. In doing so, the water must be changed each morning and placed in the sun for an hour.

The element of moving water refers to the social and business aspect of the element. When there is little movement, the persona lacks mobility and the desire to communicate with others. They prefer to stay at home and not socialize. Those with the moving water element in balance are like a river whose current flows to different lands. They like to travel and having enduring relationships. Those with too much moving water try to take advantage of every opportunity, sometimes without scruples.

To balance too much moving water, write 9 letters each day to 9 different people for 27 days, or call 9 people that you haven't spoken to in the last 6 months, for 27 days.

Those with very little of the moving water element tend not to worry, are very irresponsible and do things often without thinking. When this element is balanced, the person is sociable and has the capacity to be a good director and leader of projects and businesses. Those with too much water are emotional and demanding, any type of criticism, even constructive, angers them. They tend to be very resentful.

To harmonize the water element, we can use colors. When the water element is weak, use dark colors such as black or gray, as well as white. White corresponds to the metal element. Metal creates water. These colors stimulate the creative energy of this element, harmonizing the flow of Chi. When there is too much of the water element, use green which corresponds to wood. Wood nurtures water. Yellow and ochre are also good colors to reduce the effect of too much water.

An imbalance of the water element produces problems with the teeth, depressive states, melancholy, shivers and ear problems.

VII

THE FUNCTION OF CHI

All our actions affect society, other beings, the environment and ourselves.

Feng Shui combines many different points of view, applying methods from Hindu-Buddhist and Chinese-Confucius cultures as well as the principles of the tradition, folklore knowledge, common sense and superstition.

All living organisms move thanks to the vital life force, Chi. Chi circulates in different levels or planes of existence. We move our fingers, hands and arms because of Chi. Our bodies, organs, tissues and cells vibrate with their specific rhythms because of Chi. We view the external world and have thoughts, feelings and emotions because of Chi. If Chi does not move in our hearts, we lack the vital life-force that keeps us alive. Chi is different in each being. Chi is the true Self.

Some of the different functions of Chi are:

1. Chi helps maintain physical and mental health.
2. Chi develops mental abilities (memory, reason, visualization and concentration).
3. Chi helps personal relationships.
4. Chi develops psychic and spiritual abilities.

Each person perceives Chi in different colors in keeping with their perceptions and feelings, the same way that each crystal reflects light according their shape, structure, quality and purity.

When Chi doesn't flow as it should, it can manifest as:

1. Critical Chi
2. Dreamy Chi
3. Bamboo Chi
4. Restrictive Chi
5. Depressed Chi
6. Impulsive Chi

Critical Chi

Critical Chi manifests when someone is very talkative, a know-it-all and is given to arguments and scandals. They think that the whole world is against them and that they are not appreciated. All their problems are caused by others. Their Chi emanates as arrows to all those around them. Solution: Practice the Six True Words exercise 3 times a day.

Dreamy Chi

Dreamy Chi manifests when a person loses contact with everyday life. They are vulnerable and easily swayed. Dreamy Chi can be transformed into creative Chi if the spirit is reinforced through appropriate meditation. Solution: Practice the Six True Words exercise 9 or 27 times a day.

Bamboo Chi

Bamboo Chi makes a person inflexible, inconsiderate and demanding. These people have no time for anybody or anything; they are disorganized and tend to lose their memory and to suffer from insomnia. Solution: Place three bamboo flutes under the mattress. Bamboo flutes strengthen and protect spiritual Chi, create peace, dissipate negative energy and elevate vital life force. They also help with problems related to nerves, insomnia and back pains.

Constricted Chi

Constricted Chi manifests as insecurity and fear of speaking and acting. These people tend to have nervous attacks and psychosomatic pains. Solution: Use the Three Secrets meditation.

Depressed Chi

When depressed Chi manifests, the person feels as if their energy is completely blocked. They don't find relief from their feelings nor do they find the energy or direction to confront their problems which creates a situation of defeat and disillusionment. Solution: Place three Feng Shui flutes under the mattress and reinforce with the Three Secrets.

Impulsive Chi

Someone with impulsive Chi has aggressive energy and uses offensive language. They tend to fight, like to criticize and use their authority to take advantage of others. Solution: Place three Chinese flutes under the mattress and reinforce with the Three Secrets.

Principles of the Tradition to Elevate Chi

1. Hang a mirror on the ceiling over the bed.
2. Place three Chinese flutes under the mattress to reinforce, clarify and purify Chi.
3. Place a red banner, with the Zodiac on it, under the mattress for 9 days when you need help for important meetings or when you help others with Feng Shui.
4. To adjust Chi, peel an orange in nine circular pieces. Tear each of the 9 pieces into very small bits. Sprinkle it in each room of the house. The smell of the orange peel will strengthen and adjust the Chi of the space.
5. Say the Six True Words Mantra visualizing light and love.

VIII

SOME EXPERIENCES

On one of my trips, I was invited to do a consultation on an apartment located in a tall building built on the top of a hill. The apartment complex was a series of tall, cylindrical towers -symbolizing the wood element- trees created by modern technology.

The tradition advises that homes or living spaces be built on the sides of hills as the top of hills or mountains are subjected to inclement weather, sudden changes in the lives of those who live there, and sudden operations and accidents.

When we arrived at the apartment, we checked the location and shape of the building. Form School does not use the alignment of the space with respect to the cardinal points, but instead uses the position of the Mouth of Chi, or front door. The Mouth of Chi combines its energetic influence with the length of the wall aligned with the entrance. The Mouth of Chi determines the mystery of life itself, and symbolizes where life and the universal creative force of Chi enters the home. Life always manifests through water.

I analyzed the layout and saw that the kitchen and one of the rooms was outside the lines of harmony of the Ba-Gua. All of the apartments on this side of the building had the same design. I told the owners about this particular conflict and said that the family member who used that room would be subject to sudden changes in their lives and might leave home for some reason. As I was telling them this, their faces paled. That was their youngest son's room. They said that he was constantly depressed and always kept his room dark. But their reason for worrying was even greater than that. A few days earlier, their daughter, who also lived with them, had lost her boyfriend in an accident. The boy had lived just one floor below in an apartment with the same design. His room had been the one I pointed out as being outside the lines of harmony.

This type of energetic layout affects the lives of those who live there in different ways. In this case, a family had the sad experience of losing a son, but this does not mean that it happens in all cases. Rooms located outside the lines of harmony can be used as offices or for activities that do not have anything to do with the family or the house.

To resolve this type of conflict, the energy of the room should be integrated into the rest of the house. This can be done by hanging a mirror within the Ba-Gua of the house, on the wall facing the room, and reinforcing it with the Three Secrets.

On another occasion, when I arrived at a home, I noticed that the two small girls were fighting. Their mother told me that since they had moved into the house about a year ago, the girls had not gotten along, although this had not been the case before.

Practitioners of Feng Shui must always be aware of the small details present in a space. Shapes, colors, smells, sounds, surfaces, the surroundings, accessories, furniture, the space in general and family members manifest the state of energy or the spirit of the space. Small details sometimes produce great results. As Master Lin Yun says: "A small addition diverts and transforms adverse emanations and situations equal to thousands of tons." We should observe and be conscious of the smallest details and decorations in a home.

When I got to the girls' room, I noticed two pictures hung near the door. Each had a color photo of one of the girls taken in profile. The pictures were hung with them facing in opposite directions on either side of the door, giving the impression of separation. Remember that Chi flows according to shapes, colors and sounds. I suggested to change the position of the pictures, placing the one from the left on the right and vice versa, so that the pictures of the girls were now facing each other. In the living room, there were other pictures of people and landscapes. They were hung so the people appeared to be walking toward the door. We changed the pictures so that the people were walking «toward the house.» A few weeks later, my friends called me to say that the girls had stopped arguing. Was it due to changing the pictures or the way the furniture was arranged?

Chi is the vitalizing energy that flows through the paths of time and space. Viewing vegetation and water through doors and windows allows Chi that has entered the house to leave quickly through one of these openings back into nature. Water is the element from which life manifests and is a magnet for Chi. Houses or apartments on the ocean are subjected to these circumstances Feng Shui gives us simple methods to balance the space and energy to create a place where Chi feels good, a place of harmony. The energy of the ocean is attracted by mirrors. Mirrors hung facing it bring this source inside the space that you want to harmonize, and balances the energies inside with those outside.

When there is a lot of vegetation outside the house, plants and pictures of landscapes should be placed inside the house. We must use our knowledge of the principles of the tradition and our intuition. We should not forget to use the Nine Minor Additions, the principles of the tradition and the transcendental methods. But most importantly, as Master Thomas Lin Yun always reminds us, we should pay careful attention to our inner self which speaks to us in an intimate and subtle language through our intuition.

If you are interested in knowing more about the legendary Chinese art of Feng Shui, you can contact the following people:

Lin Yun Temple
2959 Russell Street
Berkeley CA 94705
Tel: 510-841-2347
Fax: 510-548-2621

The Fairy's Ring
73 Merrick Way
Coral Gables FL 33134
Tel: 305-446-9315
Fax: 305-448-5956
Email: fairy118@aol.com

Katherine Metz
1015 Gaily Ave, #1218
Los Angeles CA 90024
Tel: 310-208-5282
Fax: 310-208-3887

Melanie Lewandowski
PO Box 536
New Hope PA 10938-0536
Tel: 215-633-0589

The Feng Shui Warehouse
1130 Scott Street
San Diego CA 92106
Tel: 1-800-399-1599,
          619-523-2158
Fax: 619-523-2169

Feng Shui Centre
PO Box 650367
Miami, FL 33153
Email: fengshui@fengshuicom.net
Web Site: fengshuicom.net

References

Feng Shui: The Chinese Art of Placement. Sarah Rossbach.

Interior Design with Feng Shui. Sarah Rossbach.

Living Colors. Master Ling Yun and Sarah Rossbach.

Art of Placement. Katherine Metz.

Phoenix Design. Melanie Lewandowski.

Feng Shui for the Home. Evelyn Lip.

Feng Shui for Business. Evelyn Lip.

The Feng Shui Handbook. Derek Walters.

The Living Earth Manual of Feng Shui. Stephen Skinner.

Planets in Locality. Steve Cozzi.

APPENDIX

THE WHEEL OF THE EIGHT DOORS

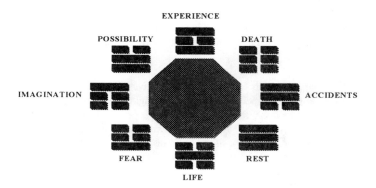

The transcendental method of the Wheel of the Eight Doors is used to clarify and reinforce the Chi of a space. It is a visualization exercise that uses two octagonal wheels, one fixed and the other moving. Each wheel consists of eight sectors or trigrams. The top wheel rotates in a succession of eight situations that can manifest within a space; which are linked with the eight predictions taught in Compass School. Form School is by nature both artistic and spiritual, and its philosophy is based on the use of traditional and transcendental methods to create harmonious spaces.

The moving wheel rotates through eight events or situations: life, accident, imagination, experience, possibility, death, fear and rest. Of these, life is the most desirable, death the least. Rest means that when things are left to pass, when no action is taken, adverse events could happen that could convert the good into bad. Imagination is linked with the creative faculty in which negative elements are transmuted from bad into good. With this adjustment, you visualize or bring "life" to all these situation or areas, and then transmute the energy of the entire space into light, life and love.

At the threshold of the house or room, imagine two octagons, one fixed and the other rotating. Before stepping into the house, feel the energy of the octagon and the space itself and try to identify which of the eight energies corresponds to it. If you feel the energy of "rest", for example, visualize "rest" transforming into "life", and then step into the house. Once inside the entrance, visualize the remaining situations rotating toward you, and transform each from negative to positive.

THE SITUATIONS OF THE WHEEL OF THE EIGHT DOORS
AND THE THEORY OF THE EIGHT PREDICTIONS

The following is a brief description of what each direction or location within a space means with regards to Compass School's Theory of the Predictions and its relationship to Form School's Theory of the Wheel of the Eight Doors. Prof. Thomas Lin Yun refers that persons are like a "living compass" and when entering through the main door in a habitat (Mouth of Ch'i) project the eight trigrams in the space with the "eight spiritual life positions" of the Ba-Gua.

The relative energy of each "direction" is what gives an area its specific meaning. This may vary depending on the specific school of Feng Shui used, and the principal point of orientation: the front door, the back door, or the personal trigram. Books written by Feng Shui masters make reference to the fact that "the conjunction of the trigrams for each direction of the space with those of the building give rise to the 'eight predictions' (mentioned below). The predictions that apply to each direction, according to different Compass School techniques, may not be apparent at first, as they are derived from the interaction of the 'First' and 'Last' sequences."

The Theory of the Eight Predictions is the most mysterious of all Feng Shui theories, especially in Compass School. The eight trigrams are divided into two groups of four: the east group, with trigrams Chen (wood) and Sun (wood) uniting Li (fire) and Kan (water) in the east; and the west group: with the Ken (earth), Kun (earth), Tui (metal) and Chien (metal) trigrams united in the west. Each group is then divided into subgroups of two trigrams: north (old trigrams) and south (young trigrams).

The above pattern establishes the Theory of the Eight Directions in the School of the Compass. Each person, and each habitat has a trigram. The group of the trigram indicates four favorable directions and four unfavorable directions.

The Personal trigram formula is calculated adding the four digits of the year of birth (if a person is born on January or February, subtract one year if born before the the Chinese New Year - See Sign Table at end of the article). The Compass Formulas for men and women are as follows:

Annual Number = Sum of the four digits of year of birth (adjusted for Chinese New Year)

Personal Trigrams

Men = 11 - Annual Number = Trigram Number
Women = Annual Number + 4 = Trigram Number

The **Trigram Numbers** correspond to the sequence established by the "Nine Star Tracing" in the Ba-Gua or Lo-Shu Table:

		S		
SUN, SE		LI		KUN, SW
	4	**9**	**2**	
CHEN, E	**3**	**5**	**7**	TUI, W
	8	**1**	**6**	
KEN, NE		KAN		CHIEN, NW
		N		

Lo-Shu Table (or Ba-Gua)

For a person born on March 3, 1960

Personal Trigram (Men) =   11 - sum digits, year of birth = 11 - 7 = 4   (Hsun, SE, Wood)
Personal Trigram (Women) = sum digits, year of birth + 4 = 7 + 4 = 11, or 2 (Kun, SW, Earth)

For a person born on Jan. 5, 1978

(Chinese New Year's started on Jan. use 1977.
Personal Trigram (Men) =   11 - 6 = 5 or 2 (Kun, SE, Earth) (5 -earth, is not a trigram. If man -Yang- uses complementary -Yin- earth trigram, or 2 - Kun, SW, Big Earth. If a woman -Yin- use complementary -Yang- earth trigram, or 8, Ken, NE, Little Earth

Personal Trigram (Women) = 6 + 4 = 10, or 1 (Kan, North, Water)

After the Personal trigram is determined, look to which Group it belongs. If the Personal trigram is in the West Group, according to the tradition, all the four directions shown in the Family Group of four trigrams Tui, Kun, Chien and Ken are favorable; in other words, the West, NW, SW and NE are favorable. If the Personal trigram is in the East Group, all the four directions shown in the Family Group of four trigrams, Chen, Sun, Li and Kan, are favorable; in other words, the East, SE, South and North directions are favorable..

The Personal trigram and the Habitat trigram belong to a group. The Personal trigram is determined by the year of birth. The Habitat trigram is determined by the magnetic compass.

Trigrams from the East Group share favorable relationships with any of the four directions corresponding to the East Group; and unfavorable relationships with any of the four directions corresponding to the West Group.

Trigrams from the West Group share favorable relationships with any of the four directions corresponding to the West Group; and unfavorable relationships with any of the four directions corresponding to the East Group.

EAST-WEST THEORY

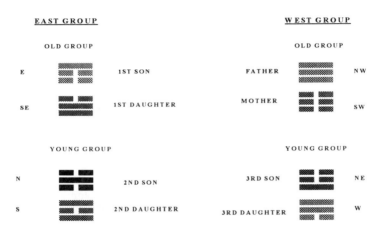

The Habitat Trigram is determined measuring the direction of the front door (or back door in some schools) with a magnetic compass, to find which of the eight directions the door is facing The measurement is taken from the inside of a habitat to the outside. Each of the eight directions corresponds with a trigram (South is Li, SW is Kun, West is Tui, NW is Chien, North is Kan, NE is Ken, East is Chen, and SE is Sun).

In accordance to the tradition, to find the favorable and unfavorble situations, the Habitat trigram or the Personal trigram is related to each of the eight directions. The Habitat trigram or Personal trigram is flown above each of the eight directions, or eight trigrams. Each relation forms a hexagram, with the Habitat or Personal trigrams "above" and the specific direction trigram of the building "below". There will be eight possible relations; four favorable and four unfavorable for each trigram; and 64 possible combinations. Each of the relations is evaluated for its positive and negative strength, in accordance to the geometrical pattern connecting the trigrams.

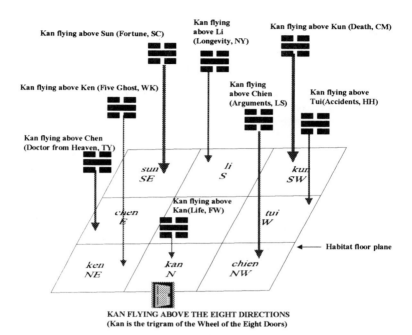

Kan flying above Sun (Fortune, SC)

Kan flying above Li (Longevity, NY)

Kan flying above Kun (Death, CM)

Kan flying above Ken (Five Ghost, WK)

Kan flying above Chien (Arguments, LS)

Kan flying above Tui(Accidents, HH)

Kan flying above Chen (Doctor from Heaven, TY)

Kan flying above Kan(Life, FW)

sun
SE

li
S

kun
SW

chen
E

tui
W

Habitat floor plane

ken
NE

kan
N

chien
NW

KAN FLYING ABOVE THE EIGHT DIRECTIONS
(Kan is the trigram of the Wheel of the Eight Doors)

THE FENG SHUI GEOMETRY OF THE EIGHT PREDICTIONS

The geometric relationships of the trigrams, among the horizontal, vertical and slanted lines connecting them, show a logical pattern that explains the eight life situations of the Wheel of the Eight Doors (Form School) and the Theory of the Eight Predictions (Compass School). The lines *connecting vertically, the same Group*, produce always favorable relationships or favorable directions. The *horizontal and slanted lines connecting East and West Groups* always produce non favorable relationships or unfavorable directions.

During my trip to Tibet in 1996, I developed the **Theory of the Sacred Geometry of the Trigrams** as it applies to both Forms and Compass Schools. This article will present the portion of the theory relating to the relationships among the eight predictions. A more detailed explanation of this theory, and how it applies more generally to Feng Shui, with complete analysis and traditional and transcendental decorative solutions is covered in my book: **The Mystical Meaning of Feng Shui**.

FAVORABLE DIRECTIONS

POSSIBILITY - SHENG CHI, VITALITY OR GENERATING BREATH (SC)

Sheng Chi is the most favorable area of space, and the best direction for a house to face or area for an office to be located. It attracts luck, fortune, prosperity and a large family. It is the best area to sleep or work in, especially for those who are in a public position. According to the energetic relationships of the trigrams in Compass School, this is the most creative position. It is an appropriate area for planning and designing projects, as well as for rest and meditation, as the harmony of this area stimulates creative intuition. This is also the best position for the front door.   Sheng Chi is always produced by vertical lines connecting a Yang to a Ying trigram of the same Group (east or west) and different subgroups (old, young).

The Sheng Chi sector is "Possibility" in the transcendental method of Form School's Wheel of the Eight Doors. The geometric relationship of the Possibility area is defined by the hexagram formed from the Spiritual Ba-Gua (or Fu Hsi Ba-Gua) trigram, Kan (Yang), on the top and the Possibility sector trigram, Sun (Yin), on the bottom (or viceversa). This combination is shown by a long vertical line that links a Yang trigram with a Yin trigram of the same group (east or west), and different subgroups (old, young).

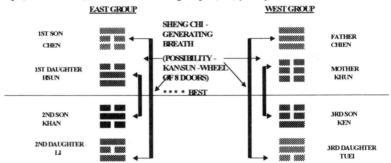

SHENG CHI - GENERATING BREATH
(POSSIBILITY - WHEEL OF 8 DOORS)

IMAGINATION - TIEN YI, FORTUNE OR CELESTIAL MONAD (TY)

Tien Yi, Celestial Monad, Tao or Doctor from Heaven, is the second best area of a space, and is considered lucky. It is a stimulating, favorable zone for important activities, sales departments, shipping goods, collections, cash registers, and all matter that deal with the financial health and personal relationships in a business. This is a favorable area for those recuperating from a sickness or for those suffering from chronic illness. It is good for a family's health to have the kitchen stove in this area. It is also ideal for the main electrical supply or fuse box (Mouth of the Chi) to be aligned with Tien Yi.

The area of Tien Yi is "Imagination" in the transcendental method of Form School's the Wheel of the Eight Doors. The geometric relationship of Imagination is defined by the hexagram formed from the Spiritual Ba-Gua trigram, Kan, on the top and the Imagination sector trigram, Sun, on the bottom. This combination is shown by a medium-length, vertical line that links two Yang trigrams or two Yin trigrams of the same group (east or west), and different subgroups (old, young).

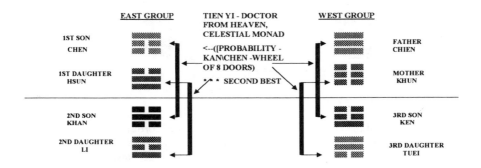

EXPERIENCE - NIEN YEN, LONGEVITY (NY)

Nien Yen is the third best positions among the four favorable positions within a space. This area reflects positive energy that manifests as prosperity, and is related to long life and harmonious marital and familial relationships. This area can be used for business administration or management, or for activities that influence the success of a business such as accounting offices, supervision, etc. Feng Shui masters recommend that this area be used to harmonize and unite family members, as its energy improves the quality of life, and personal relationships and communication. According to the tradition, this area can help resolve personality conflicts and family problems. Marital difficulties can be alleviated, improved or solved by locating the bedroom in this area of the house.

The Nien Yen sector is "Experience" in the transcendental method of Form School's the Wheel of the Eight Doors. The geometric relationship of the Experience area is defined by the hexagram formed from the Spiritual Ba-Gua trigram, Kan, on the top and the Experience sector trigram, Li, on the bottom. This combination is shown by a short vertical line that links a Yang trigram with a Yin trigram of the same group (east or west), and same subgroup (old, young).

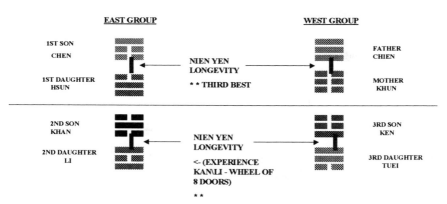

LIFE - FU WEI, LIFE (FW)

Fu Wei is the fourth of the favorable areas of a space. This area corresponds to the direction of the front door. Life enters through the main door, or as it is known in Form School, the "Mouth of Chi". It is a favorable direction for obtaining peace and harmony, which improves the quality of life at home and at work. This area can be honored with decorations, paintings or ornamental objects that stimulate life and reflect the water element.

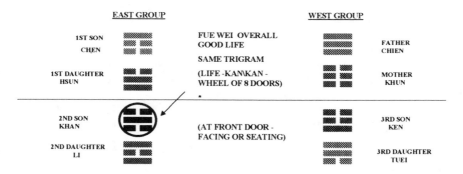

The Fu Wei sector is "Life" in the transcendental method of Form School's the Wheel of the Eight Doors. The geometric relationship of the Life area is defined the hexagram formed from the Spiritual Ba-Gua trigram, Kan, on the top and the trigram of the entrance, Kan. This combination forms a hexagram which, according to the Theory of the Sacred Geometry of the Trigrams, is represented by the circle, a symbol of harmony and life.

UNFAVORABLE DIRECTIONS

DEATH - CHUE MING, DEATH OR PAINFUL DESTINY (CM)

Chue Ming is the worst area within a space. It is the most dangerous area for businesses as well as homes. According to the tradition, Chue Ming can cause the loss of possessions, family and health. Try to avoid this sector at all costs, especially when performing activities that are physically challenging or risky. This area can be used for storage or inventory. Feng Shui, Compass School practitioners always examine this area carefully, and many times suggest moving out from this area, or relocation of door to change the energy situation. Other solutions include locating the bathroom here to dissipate the negative influences produced by Chue Ming. Having the kitchen in this area is also recommended, provided that the stove is aligned with a favorable direction.. Other methods include use of concave mirrors, transformation of Chue Ming by incense offerings, transcendental reinforcement for protection, Tracing the Nine Stars, The Wheel of the Eight Doors and techniques from the Theory of the 24 Stars.

The Chue Ming sector is "Death" in the transcendental method of Form School's the Wheel of the Eight Doors. The geometric relationship of the Death area is defined by the hexagram formed from the Spiritual Ba-Gua trigram, Kan, on the top and the Death sector trigram, Kun, on the bottom. This combination is shown by a slanted line (large cross) that links a Yang trigram with a Yin trigram of different groups (east with west), and different subgroups (north, south).

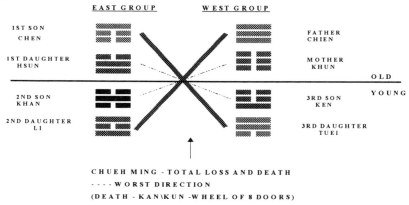

CHUEH MING - TOTAL LOSS AND DEATH
- - - - WORST DIRECTION
(DEATH - KAN\KUN -WHEEL OF 8 DOORS)

REST - LUI SHA, THE SIX CURSES, THE SEVEN LITTLE DEVILS (LS)

Lui Sha, or the "six curses", is the second worst position and an area of bad luck and negative influences that produces frustration and depression. According to the tradition, it produces conflict, arguments, fights, legal problems, enemies, betrayal and loss of opportunities at work or in business. It is not an appropriate area to negotiate financial activities, or for an office of a manager or administrator, as it could cause financial problems. Law suits, legal problems, accidents could occur frequently at home and at work, which could at times be the cause of chronic illness and death. This area should be used for inventory, office supplies, printers, etc. A toilet in this area diminishes and weakens the negative effect of Lui Sha. Other methods include transcendental techniques, Tracing the Nine Stars, The Wheel of the Eight Doors.

The Lui Sha sector is "Rest" in the transcendental method of Form School's the Wheel of the Eight Doors. "Rest" means just letting things happen, both negative events as well as positive, so in this sense, "Rest" is not good. The geometric relationship of the Rest area is defined by the hexagram formed from the Spiritual Ba-Gua trigram, Kan, on the top and the Rest sector trigram, Chien, on the bottom. This combination is shown by a slanted line that links two Yang trigrams, or two Yin trigram of different groups (east with west), and different subgroups (north, south).

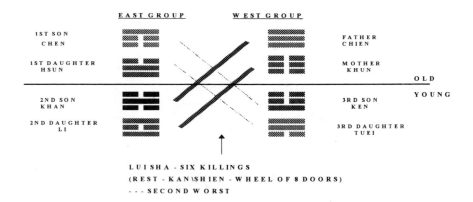

ACCIDENTS - HO HAI, ACCIDENTS OR MISFORTUNE (HH).

Ho Hai is the third of the worst predictions within a space. This location can produce accidents or sudden changes in a person's life. Using this area can affect the inhabitant's financial situation or be the cause of lost friendships or legal cases. This is the most accident-prone area within a space, so risky activities should be avoided. It is not advisable to have objects, machinery, or dangerous tools here without taking the necessary precautions. This area can be used as storage.

The Ho Hai sector is "Accident" in the transcendental method of Form School's the Wheel of the Eight Doors. The geometric relationship of the Accident area is defined by the hexagram formed from the Spiritual Ba-Gua trigram, Kan, on top and the Accident sector trigram, Tui, on the bottom. This combination is shown by a slanted line (small cross) that links a Yang trigram with a Yin trigram of different groups (east with west), and the same subgroup (north, south).

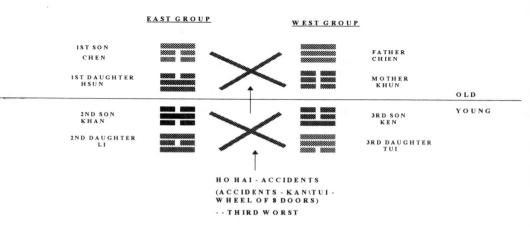

EAST GROUP   WEST GROUP

1ST SON CHEN   FATHER CHIEN

1ST DAUGHTER HSUN   MOTHER KHUN

OLD

YOUNG

2ND SON KHAN   3RD SON KEN

2ND DAUGHTER LI   3RD DAUGHTER TUI

HO HAI - ACCIDENTS
(ACCIDENTS - KAN\TUI -
WHEEL OF 8 DOORS)
- - THIRD WORST

FEAR - WU KUEI, SPIRIT OR THE FIVE GHOSTS (WK)

This is a spiritual area related to honoring ancestors, similar to the Family area in Form School, and is an appropriate area to honor the spirit of ancestors, or people who have passed on. It is also a good area for meditation and requesting help from spiritual entities, as long as the energy it represents is honored properly. It is an area of bad luck, and is the second worst position within a space. It is not an advisable to have a bedroom in this area.

This direction can produce emotional problems and nervous states, as well as spiritual uneasiness and uncertainty that can lead to depression. A door in this area could be the cause of robberies, fire, and in some cases, problems with the youngest child in the family. The influence of Wu Kuei can lead to hidden enemies, misunderstanding among members of the family, friends and co-workers. To adjust or negate the negative effects of Wu Kuei, place a toilet in this area.

The Wu Kuei sector is "Fear" in the transcendental method of Form School's the Wheel of the Eight Doors. The geometric relationship of the Fear area is defined by the hexagram formed from the Spiritual Ba-Gua trigram, Kan, on the top and the Fear sector trigram, Ken, on the bottom. This combination is shown by a horizontal line that links two Yang trigrams, or two Yin trigrams of different groups (east with west).

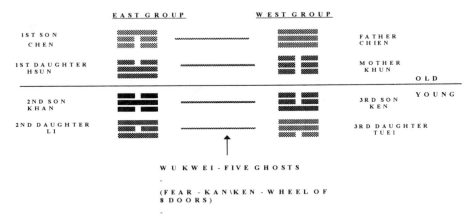

WU KWEI - FIVE GHOSTS

(FEAR - KAN\KEN - WHEEL OF 8 DOORS)

The Geometry of the Trigrams of the I-Ching

The Theory of the Predictions of Feng Shui is based on the trigrams as well as the directions. The Theory of the Sacred Geometry of the Trigrams uses the geometric relationships of the trigrams to explain where or in what direction each of the predictions is found. This geometric relationship is a function of the trigram of the front door (regardless of the method used: front door, back door or personal trigram).

THE THEORY OF THE EIGHT PREDICTIONS

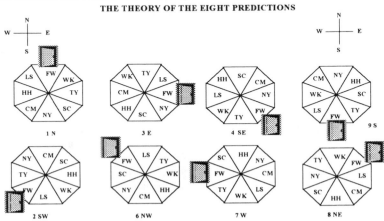

First, the trigram of the persons or space is determined, then it is used in conjunction with each one of the directional trigrams to form an individual hexagram, for a total of eight hexagrams: the upper trigram is the trigram of the habitat (or personal trigram) and the lower trigram is determined by each of the eight compass directions. The lines that connect the trigrams of the hexagram, based on an east-west orientation, determine the situation or prediction of each of the areas of the space.

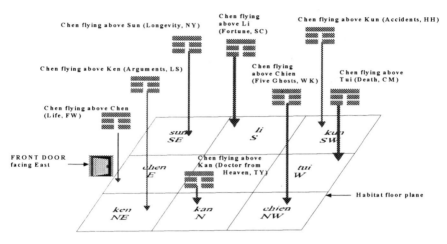

CHEN FLYING ABOVE THE EIGHT DIRECTIONS

When using the geometric method, conventional tables are not needed to determine each area or prediction; you need only to draw the trigrams, and the geometric relationships between the trigrams. The vertical lines and the circle, which connect two trigrams of the same group, always represent favorable relationships or directions. Slanted or horizontal lines connecting two trigrams of different groups represent unfavorable predictions or directions.

SC - SHENG CHI GENERATING BREATH
TY - DOCTOR FROM HEAVEN
NY- NIEN YEN - LONGEVITY
FW - FU WEI - HARMONIOUS LIFE

CM - CHUE MING - TOTAL LOSS
LS - LUI SHA - SIX KILLINGS
HH - HO HAI - ACCIDENTS
WK - WU KWEI - FIVE GHOSTS

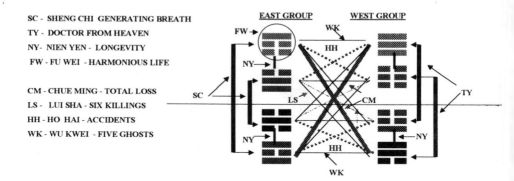

THE SPIRITUAL BA-GUA

Form School's transcendental method of the Wheel of the Eight Doors always uses Kan as the trigram of the space. In keeping with the spiritual nature of Form School, life always manifests through water, and thus the main door of a space or building is always aligned with the line of water and the trigram Kan. A human being is like a "living compass" proyecting the Spiritual Ba-Gua in the spaces, through the main entrace (Mouth of Chi).

THE METHODS TO COMPLEMENT FORMS AND COMPASS SCHOOLS METHODS AND SOLUTIONS FOR UNFAVORABLE COMPASS DIRECTIONS ARE COVERED EXTENSIVELY IN THE BOOK **"THE MYSTICAL MEANING OF FENG SHUI"**.

八卦

雲石精舍主人林鶖之題
七一

Index